E. M. Forster's

A Passage To India

Text by
Ann Wood
(M.A. Columbia University)
Department of Writing & Speech
New York City Technical College
Brooklyn, New York

Illustrations by
Karen Pica

 Research & Education Association

MAXnotes® for
A PASSAGE TO INDIA

Printed in the United States of America

Library of Congress Catalog Card Number 96-67434

International Standard Book Number 0-87891-039-5

MAXnotes® is a registered trademark of
Research & Education Association, Piscataway, New Jersey 08854

What **MAXnotes**® *Will Do for You*

This book is intended to help you absorb the essential contents and features of E. M. Forster's *A Passage To India* and to help you gain a thorough understanding of the work. The book has been designed to do this more quickly and effectively than any other study guide.

For best results, this **MAXnotes** book should be used as a companion to the actual work, not instead of it. The interaction between the two will greatly benefit you.

To help you in your studies, this book presents the most up-to-date interpretations of every section of the actual work, followed by questions and fully explained answers that will enable you to analyze the material critically. The questions also will help you to test your understanding of the work and will prepare you for discussions and exams.

Meaningful illustrations are included to further enhance your understanding and enjoyment of the literary work. The illustrations are designed to place you into the mood and spirit of the work's settings.

The **MAXnotes** also include summaries, character lists, explanations of plot, and section-by-section analyses. A biography of the author and discussion of the work's historical context will help you put this literary piece into the proper perspective of what is taking place.

The use of this study guide will save you the hours of preparation time that would ordinarily be required to arrive at a complete grasp of this work of literature. You will be well prepared for classroom discussions, homework, and exams. The guidelines that are included for writing papers and reports on various topics will prepare you for any added work which may be assigned.

The **MAXnotes** will take your grades "to the max."

Dr. Max Fogiel
Program Director

Contents

> **Each chapter includes List of Characters,
> Summary, Analysis, Study Questions and
> Answers, and Suggested Essay Topics.**

SECTION ONE

Introduction

The Life and Work of E. M. Forster

Edward Morgan Forster was born in London on January 1, 1879. After graduating from Tonbridge School, he attended King's College, Cambridge where he was exposed to the values of liberal humanism and discovered an appreciation of the human being as an individual and the value of friendship. Many of the friendships he made at Cambridge were lasting ones, and he was later to travel to India for the first time with university friends.

Forster's literary career began in 1903, when he began writing for *The Independent Review*, a liberal and anti-imperialist publication that he co-founded with Lowes Dickinson. He soon published his first novel, *Where Angels Fear to Tread* (1905); by 1910, he had written three more. *The Longest Journey* (1907), *A Room with a View* (1908), and *Howard's End* (1910) exhibit a growth in the novelist's skill and in the range of his subjects. In *A Room with a View*, which is set first in Florence and then in English suburbia, Forster reveals himself as a critic of social snobbery and suburban pretension.

In addition to their observation of social codes, all of Forster's novels portray sensitive characters struggling with the inflexibility of these codes and the insensitivity of those around them. Although Forster's point of view is often comic and ironic, his characters' personal feelings are usually presented as serious, or at key moments, sacred. This is especially apparent in Forster's last novel, *A Passage to India*, first published in 1924. *A Passage to India* is the novelist's acknowledged masterpiece.

Although Forster was born and raised in England, and lived much of his life there, travel was an important element in his life and work. During World War I, he obtained a position with the Red Cross in Alexandria, Egypt. By this time Forster was already an established and recognized writer. Forster's life and career spanned many historical changes, including two world wars and the dismantling of much of the British Empire. He observed the British colonial administration first-hand in 1912, when he made the long journey by sea to India. After this trip, he wrote most of the first section of *A Passage to India*, but it was not until after a second visit, in 1921, when he spent six months as private secretary to a Hindu Maharajah, that he completed it. His masterpiece was published in 1924 and unanimously praised by literary critics. Members of the British colonial society in England were less enthusiastic. They criticized its portrayal of the colonial adminis- trators, while some Indians wrote that he had misunderstood the Indian characters or treated them condescendingly. However, Forster's goal was not to produce a documentary portrayal of India or Indian society; for example, he changed the names of Indian towns and regions, even inventing his own Marabar Caves in place of the actual Ajanta Caves. Instead of drawing a portrait of a country, he was presenting an overall impression that continually emphasized the way in which the inner qualities of certain individuals and universal feelings were restricted by social, religious, and ethnic codes. Above all, his novel dramatically depicted the deep spiritual tensions of two clashing civilizations: the East and the West.

After *A Passage to India*, his greatest success, Forster never wrote another novel. He turned, instead, to short stories, essays, and biographies. In 1925, he was awarded the Tait Black Memorial and femina Vie Heureuse prizes. Forster never married and he died in 1970. It was not until the year after his death that his 1914 novel *Maurice* was published for the first time.

Beginning with the Oscar-winning film of *A Passage to India*, which appeared in 1984, Forster's popularity has increased. David Lean's version of *A Passage to India* was followed by the Merchant-Ivory productions of *A Room with a View* and *Howard's End*, in 1987 and 1992, respectively. The success of these films has led to a renewed appreciation of Forster's gift for portraying the complex inner lives of his characters and the rigid, yet temporary, nature of the social structures they inhabit.

Historical Background

The political structure of the India that Forster visited and depicted in *A Passage to India* over 70 years ago was fundamentally different from that of India today. In Forster's day, India was ruled by the British. It had not yet won its independence, nor had it endured the partition and savage rioting that followed it. Forster's India was one country, not yet separated into India and Pakistan. The caste system, a strict social categorization that would later be attacked and weakened by Mahatma Gandhi and others, still ruled Hindu life and culture.

The India of Forster's novel is still recognizable as a huge, hot, sprawling country, home to a multitude of ethnic groups and religions. Some 200 languages are spoken there. Religious and spiritual life seem to play a different, more open and imposing role in India than in the West. The major religions are Hindu and Muslim, with important minorities such as Sikhs and Parsis. The overall impression is one of diversity, sometimes accompanied by tolerance and sometimes by riots and massacres, during which one group attacks another or destroys sacred sites associated with another tradition.

A Passage to India is set in India under what was known as the British Raj, a system of colonial administration that began in a few coastal states as an outgrowth of the British East India Company. It grew to include almost all of India. The British East India Company's major trade was in cotton goods, silks, spices, and saltpeter. Throughout the seventeenth and eighteenth centuries, aided by the British army and its Indian contingents, the Company extended its power and profits in India. In 1858, after the Indian Mutiny, the Company came under the direct rule of the British crown.

Although the mutiny is mentioned occasionally in Forster's novel, it remains a ghostly presence and a reminder of a time when the subjects rose up against the representatives of the foreign power in their midst. The shock of the uprisings that took place in various parts of India, during which people were shot or hacked to death, reverberated in the memory of the English colonialists, while Indians never forgot the revolting punishments imposed when the mutiny was put down and the British Army took its revenge. Another and more recent massacre had occurred in the Punjab in 1919, between Forster's first and second trip to India, when hundreds of peaceful Sikh demonstrators were shot down by the British Army at Amritsar.

Deeply shocked by the reports from Amritsar, Forster condemned the massacre as an example of "public infamy." It was the slaughter of the nationalist demonstrators at Amritsar, as well as Britain's hostility toward the Khilafat, an Islamic movement, which led Hindus and Muslims to join in a non-cooperation movement. Although Forster lived in the Hindu state of Dewas during his second visit to India, he was aware that this movement was growing rapidly in British India, and was producing marked changes in the Indian social and political scene. Besides protesting against imperialism, social discrimination, and repression, the native inhabitants of the country were attempting to regain control of their own destinies. *A Passage to India* depicts the conditions under which Indians were deprived of opportunities for advancement and were continually overlooked or insulted by the Anglo-Indian ruling class.

A specific historical situation that Forster probably employed in constructing the central incident in *A Passage to India* had occurred in Amritsar in 1919, around the time of the massacre. It was written by "an Englishwoman" who was new to India and had lived in Amritsar at the time of the nationalist demonstrations. In her article, published in *Blackwood's Magazine* in April 1920, she describes an occasion on which an English girl had been brutally assaulted by a group of Indians. In the aftermath, the Anglo-Indians gathered at the Fort and special trains took the women to the hills, just as in the novel. Forster may well have read this Englishwoman's account and based parts of *A Passage to India* on it. Various other features of the historical events, including the conciliatory tactics adopted by the British authorities after the crisis, seem to be reflected or referred to in the novel.

When seen against the historical background of British rule in India, the events of the novel take on greater resonance. For example, in the context of punishments that had actually been inflicted on

Indians—such as the "crawling order" that forced them to crawl on all fours through a particular lane after the Amritsar assault—the bitter vengefulness expressed by some Anglo-Indian characters in the novel cannot be attributed simply to individual aberrations. Revenge had become an instrument of government policy. Similarly, the Indians' deep distrust of their British rulers, which at times seems to border on paranoia, can be understood as a reaction to the system of apartheid instituted by the British Raj.

Master List of Characters

Dr. Aziz—*Muslim surgeon, works under Major Callendar; accused by Miss Quested; becomes a friend of Fielding.*

Hamidullah—*Muslim friend and relative by marriage of Aziz, prominent Chandrapore barrister; aspires to social contact with the English but is aware of the difficulties.*

Mahmoud Ali—*Muslim lawyer, friend of Hamidullah and Aziz; a troublemaker who is constantly spreading malicious rumors.*

Mohammed Latif—*Muslim, poor relation of Hamidullah, neither servant nor equal.*

Mrs. Moore—*Older woman, sensitive to the soul of India, friendly to Aziz and Miss Quested, mother of Ronny Heaslop, later becomes known as a Hindu Goddess; Esmiss Esmoor.*

Major Callendar—*The civil surgeon, Aziz's superior but not as good a doctor, disrespectful toward Indians and ignorant of Indian life.*

Ronny Heaslop—*The city magistrate, Mrs. Moore's son, insecure, wants to do his duty but bewildered by India; becomes Miss Quested's fiancé.*

Miss Adela Quested—*Intellectual, considered unattractive, thinks with her head rather than her heart, close to Mrs. Moore; becomes engaged to Ronny Heaslop, accuser of Aziz, confides in Fielding.*

Mr. Turton—*The collector, a civil servant.*

Mrs. Turton—*Insensitive, used to giving orders, at first conventionally prejudiced, later furiously authoritarian and vengeful.*

Cyril Fielding—*Principal of Government College at Chandrapore; looked down on by Anglo-Indians, becomes friend of Aziz, helps Miss Quested after the trial, later marries Mrs. Moore's daughter, Stella.*

Nawab Bahadur—*Muslim, referred to as the "geyser," wealthy proprietor and philanthropist, grandfather of Nureddin, haunted by a ghost.*

Mr. Ram Chand—*Hindu associate of Dr. Panna Lal.*

Mr. Graysford and Mr. Sorley—*Anglo-Indian missionaries.*

Miss Nancy Derek—*Assistant to a Maharani in Native State, crude, talkative, makes fun of Indians, having an affair with the magistrate, McBryde.*

McBryde—*District Superintendent of Police, tough-minded, most reflective and best educated of the officials.*

Mrs. McBryde—*His wife.*

Mr. and Mrs. Bhattacharya—*Hindus of some wealth and status.*

Dr. Panna Lal—*Low-caste Hindu, fellow-assistant but not friend of Aziz, something of a caricature.*

A Subaltern—*Anglo-Indian army officer of lower rank.*

Professor Narayan Godbole—*Hindu, a Deccani Brahmin of the highest caste, elderly, scholarly; his name suggests "God man of God," a philosopher and devotee of Shri Krishna, acquaintance of Aziz and his Muslim friends, and of Fielding.*

Mr. Harris—*The Eurasian chauffer.*

Krishna—*An attendant in Heaslop's office.*

Nureddin—*The Nawab Bahadur's grandson, at first beautiful, later mutilated in an accident.*

Hassan—*Aziz's servant.*

Syed Mohammed—*An engineer.*

Mr. Haq—*Indian police inspector, at first friendly with Aziz, later arrests him.*

Rafi—*Student of Fielding's, called the "Sherlock Holmes of Chandrapore" because of his love of gossip and rumor.*

Antony—*Servant of Mrs. Moore and Miss Quested, considers himself of a higher class than other servants.*

A Young Mother—*Blonde Englishwoman; symbolizes British womanhood.*

Mr. Amritrao—*Oxford-educated Calcutta barrister, notoriously anti-British; Aziz's lawyer at the trial.*

Lady Mellanby—*Wife of the lieutenant-governor of the providence.*

Sir Gilbert Mellanby—*Lieutenant governor of the providence.*

The punkah-wallah—*A fan attendant, divinely beautiful, does not speak, a force of nature.*

Mr. Das—*Hindu judge nominally in charge of Aziz's trial; Heaslop's assistant.*

Shri Krishna—*Hindu deity, incarnate god of love and wisdom; center of Gokul Ashtami festival in celebration of his August birthday.*

Major Roberts—*The new civil surgeon.*

Young Milner—*The new city magistrate.*

Rajah of Mau—*Hindu ruler of an independent Native State where Dr. Aziz and Professor Godbole are living at the end of the novel.*

Colonel Maggs—*British political agent in Mau who attempts to harass Aziz.*

Ralph Moore—*Mrs. Moore's son, Stella's brother, Fielding's brother-in-law, intimidated and then embraced by Aziz.*

Stella (Moore) Fielding—*Mrs. Moore's daughter, then Fielding's wife, she is spiritually in tune with India and inwardly tranquil.*

Jemila, Ahmed, and Karim—*Aziz's children.*

Summary of the Novel

A Passage to India begins in the town of Chandrapore. The first section, entitled *Mosque*, introduces a gathering of Muslim friends who are discussing the problem of friendship with the Anglo-Indians, their British rulers. Among them is Dr. Aziz, a surgeon, who afterwards has a fateful meeting in a mosque with Mrs. Moore. Their conversation brings them close and later she introduces him to her younger friend, Miss Quested, who has arrived to marry Mrs. Moore's son.

Various attempts are made to bridge the gap between the Indians and the English: an awkward mixed "bridge-party" at the English Club; Aziz's brief experience of fellowship while playing polo with a subaltern; and an "unconventional" gathering of the Muslim Aziz, the Hindu Professor Godbole, Mrs. Moore, and Mrs. Quested at a teaparty at Fielding's house. The relative success of the tea party inspires Aziz to invite all present to accompany him on a planned excursion to the Marabar Caves.

Miss Quested decides not to marry Ronny Heaslop, but then changes her mind and they become engaged. Driving in a car with the Nawab Bahadur, they have an accident; this draws them together and they announce their engagement to Mrs. Moore. Meanwhile, rumors, suspicion, and mutual rancor between Muslims and Hindus emerge in a gathering attended by Aziz, Dr. Panna Lal, and others, though they maintain a superficial politeness.

In the second section, *The Caves*, Aziz's excursion begins. Fielding and Professor Godbole are delayed and do not join Aziz and the two women on the train. Once in the caves, Mrs. Moore is disoriented and overcome by incomprehensible sensations. She leaves the caves. Aziz and Miss Quested continue, but after she asks an annoying question, he leaves her and goes into another cave. When he emerges, he sees her far down the hill. Fielding, who is just arriving, asks about Miss Quested. Instead of telling the truth, Aziz invents a story. When they return to Chandrapore, Aziz is arrested. Miss Quested has charged him with attempting to "insult" her in the caves. This is clearly a euphemism for a sexual advance or attack.

The British community is furious and indignant; Aziz is denied bail. Fielding's attempts to speak to Adela Quested fail. Mrs. Moore refuses to remain in India to testify at the trial. She books passage on a ship for England. Miss Quested tells her fiancé that Aziz is innocent, but Heaslop will not do anything about it. At the trial, when she finally takes the witness stand, she admits that she was mistaken about the supposed assault. The Muslims stage a march to celebrate Aziz's release. Fielding rescues Miss Quested by taking her to his garden house. There, they learn that Mrs. Moore has died at sea, before the trial. Ronny Heaslop breaks his engagement to Adela, who leaves for England. Fielding resigns from the Club. Aziz has begun to distrust Fielding; he believes that Fielding is trying to keep Miss Quested from paying compensation and even that he is having a secret affair with her.

The third and final section, *The Temple*, takes place years later. Professor Godbole and Aziz are now living and working in the Native State of Mau, ruled by an aging Rajah. The section opens with Professor Godbole, who is now minister of education in Mau, and soon leads into the Gokul Ashtami, a great festival celebrating the birthday of Shri Krishna. There, Professor Godbole dances in worship of the god and remembers Mrs. Moore with love. Aziz has refused to read Fielding's letters, still imagining that he has married Miss Quested. When Fielding arrives in his role as inspector of education, he attempts to make peace with Aziz, pointing out that his wife is not Miss Quested but Mrs. Moore's daughter, Stella. Stella and her brother, Ralph, have come to India with him. Aziz at first treats Ralph roughly, but then, remembering Mrs. Moore, he softens toward him. The Rajah has died, although his death is being concealed. Aziz and Fielding go for a last ride together and recapture much of their old intimacy. Yet Aziz insists that the British must be forced out, so that India will be a sovereign nation. Fielding disagrees. Although the two men want to be friends, the historical circumstances do not allow for friendship between them.

Estimated Reading Time

The average reader may wish to dedicate at least six hours to *A Passage to India*, in order to become accustomed to the exotic setting, the large cast of characters with their ethnic backgrounds, and the intricacies of both British and Indian social systems. (A glossary of Anglo-Indian terms is provided in the appendix of this study guide.) It is essential to pay close attention to the three-part division of the novel, and to consider the title of each section and how it relates to individual chapters.

The first section concentrates on identifying and distinguishing individual characters, their contrasting backgrounds, and the differences and similarities between them. Themes of sex and marriage, and of ghosts and secrets make their appearance, and the great theme of kindness between cultures and between individuals is emphasized at the end.

The next section is introduced by a description of the mystical and symbolic Marabar Caves. This section constitutes the heart of the novel and presents its principal dramatic and thematic content. The climax of the novel occurs when Aziz's trial takes place. This scene should be read carefully, both for its theatrical quality and its resolution. The end of the *Caves* section presents the aftermath of the trial and emphasizes the themes of death and departure.

A final, short section begins two years later. Its chapters can easily be read as a single unit, with particular attention to the scene of Professor Godbole dancing at the Krishna festival and the confrontation between Fielding and Aziz in the book's final scene.

A Passage to India

Part I: Mosque
Chapters I – III

New Characters:

Dr. Aziz: *Muslim surgeon working under Major Callendar*

Hamidullah: *Muslim, prominent Chandrapore barrister*

Mahmoud Ali: *Muslim lawyer, a troublemaker*

Mohammed Latif: *Hamidullah's relative and hanger-on*

Major Callendar: *English, the civil surgeon*

Mrs. Moore: *older Englishwoman visiting India, mother of Ronny*

Ronny Heaslop: *English, the city magistrate*

Miss Adela Quested: *young Englishwoman visiting India*

Mr. Turton: *English civil servant, the collector*

Mrs. Turton: *his wife*

Cyril Fielding: *Principal of Government College at Chandrapore*

Summary

There is a description of the town of Chandrapore and its tri-partite division into Indian, Eurasian, and English sections. The larger setting dominates: the river Ganges, vegetation, the sky and

the sun, and, 20 miles to the south, the Marabar Hills and their fabled caves.

In Chapter II, Aziz and Mahmoud Ali gather at Hamidullah's house and discuss the topic of friendship between Indians and the English. Hamidullah takes Aziz into the *purdah* quarters to see his wife, who raises the question of whether Aziz will marry again. When they finally sit down to dinner, they are interrupted by a servant who bears a note summoning Aziz to the bungalow of Major Callendar. Aziz reluctantly sets out. When he reaches the bungalow, the Major is not at home and Aziz's *tonga* is commandeered by the Major's wife and her friend Mrs. Lesley. Aziz begins to walk back, stopping off in a mosque at the edge of the civil station, where he thinks of Persian poetry and encounters Mrs. Moore. After his initial anger, they begin a pleasant conversation, interrupted by an angry outburst in which Aziz complains about the way Major Callendar and his wife treat him. He escorts Mrs. Moore back to the Club, and explains to her that Indians are not allowed inside.

Chapter III is set in the Club, where Mrs. Moore is greeted by Adela Quested. The performance of *Cousin Kate* is ending. The Anglo-Indians begin to talk about the "real India." Someone passing by (Fielding), suggests: "Try seeing Indians." Most of the women find this idea outlandish, and begin to talk of the need to maintain a distance from the natives. Mr. Turton offers to arrange a social meeting with Indians for Mrs. Moore. Mr. and Mrs. Turton depart; so do Ronny Heaslop, Miss Quested and Mrs. Moore, who tells her son about her encounter in the mosque. Heaslop is disturbed, and lectures his mother about mingling with the natives. They pause by the luminous Ganges. At home, Mrs. Moore and her son discuss Aziz's motives. Heaslop agrees not to mention Aziz's conversation in the mosque to Major Callendar. In return, he asks Mrs. Moore not to speak of it to Miss Quested, who is in India to decide whether or not to marry him.

Analysis

The first chapter of the novel creates a large canvas that emphasizes the overwhelming power of nature—the river Ganges, the creeping vegetation, the sky and distance beyond stars, and the far hills with their suggestion of mysterious caves. By concentrating entirely on the natural background without depicting a single human figure, it is suggested that human life is relatively puny and ephemeral.

The next subject is human social arrangements and the mutual distrust and misunderstandings that arise within relatively closed societies. The focus shifts to a particular human social arrangement—the social life of Muslims in Chandrapore. Among themselves, they seem affectionate and convivial, yet when they discuss the English, the gulf that divides the two groups becomes evident. Instead of complaining about the discrimination in rank and pay scale, as we might expect, they are troubled by the denial of friendship and social intercourse. It is clear from the Muslims' conversation that when the English come to live in India, they quickly learn that they have the right, or the duty, to snub even a Cambridge-educated Indian lawyer like Hamidullah.

Women occupy a particular place in each group. Hamidullah invites Aziz into the *purdah* quarters to visit his wife, Begum Hamidullah. Among the Muslims, the women live in separate quarters and are only seen by visitors when the male head of the household issues an invitation.

In some ways, Anglo-Indian social life is quite different. Mrs. Lesley and Mrs. Turton, unescorted by their husbands, commandeer a *tonga* and drive off to the Club, where men and women mingle freely and drink together. The women express their opinions and enforce social conformity as fiercely as the men.

Anglo-Indian men have high-sounding titles like chief magistrate, controller, and chief surgeon. They are the heads of departments, and even highly qualified Indians who work there are subordinate in rank and salary. These Indians are barred from the Club, the center of social life in the Anglo-Indian civil station at Chandrapore; they may only enter the gardens.

Yet the two groups are forced into an acute awareness of each other. While the Muslims seem to long wistfully for greater contact and even friendship, the majority of the Anglo-Indians are determined to maintain a wide social gulf. They are convinced that they understand the Indians and seem always to believe the worst of them. Each group is suspicious of the others' motives.

One of the novel's most important themes, the importance of human sensitivity, is introduced during the conversation between Aziz and Mrs. Moore. Aziz tells Mrs. Moore that she knows what others feel. In this, he maintains, she is an Oriental. The contrast is between the "typical" Anglo-Indian insensitive analytical approach and the "typical" Oriental sensitivity and responsiveness. Yet within each group, there will be exceptions. This emphasis on sensitivity to other's feelings—or lack of it—will recur in many other scenes.

Potential tensions between conformist and nonconformist Anglo-Indians are suggested when an enigmatic figure appears briefly at the Club. This is Fielding, who becomes the protagonist of the novel. His heretical suggestion ("Try meeting Indians") runs directly counter to the prevailing opinion of the others at the Club. He is thus already something of an outsider, one who defies group opinion and is therefore considered eccentric or unacceptable. In contrast, Ronny Heaslop is doing his best to conform to his responsibilities within Anglo-Indian society, although he is not entirely convinced that its values are correct. His attempt to rebuke Mrs. Moore for her excursion to the mosque provides an example of the way social controls are exercised in order to produce uniform attitudes and behavior.

The appearance of the wasp at the end of Chapter III briefly returns us to the world of nature, this time in miniature. The novelist introduces an ironic note here, when Mrs. Moore says naively, "Pretty wasp." Since wasps are famed for fierceness rather than beauty, this suggests that Mrs. Moore may have some unpleasant surprises ahead of her. Mrs. Moore notes that this is not an English wasp—and Forster remarks that in India, insects and animals do not distinguish between trees and houses, finding both an outgrowth of the eternal jungle. Once again, we are reminded of the world of nature that surrounds and dwarfs all social groupings. The chapter ends with a foreshadowing of things to come, the word "uneasiness."

Study Questions

1. Where are the Marabar Caves in relation to Chandrapore?
2. What does Hamidullah believe about the possibility of friendship with the English in India?

3. Why do Mrs. Turton and Mrs. Lesley not ask Aziz if they may take the *tonga*?

4. Why does Aziz find it possible to talk freely to Mrs. Moore? What is her attitude toward the Indians?

5. What is Ronny Heaslop's reaction when he discovers his mother has been talking to Dr. Aziz?

6. What does Mr. Turton mean when he says that Heaslop's a *sahib*?

7. What kind of a "bridge-party" does Mr. Turton intend to give?

8. Why do the Englishwomen feel it is necessary to keep a distance from the Indians?

9. How does Fielding's attitude differ from that of his fellow Anglo-Indians?

10. Why does Aziz resent Major Callendar?

Answers

1. The Marabar Caves are 20 miles from Chandrapore, set in the Marabar Hills, which can be seen from the city.

2. Hamidullah believes that it may be possible to have a friendship with the English in India under certain conditions.

3. Mrs. Turton and Mrs. Lesley, like most other Anglo-Indians, are used to ignoring native Indians and their rights or interests. They turn their heads away from Aziz as if he did not exist.

4. He finds her sensitive to the feelings of others. Mrs. Moore is surprised and disturbed by Heaslop's harsh judgment of Indians. She is eager to meet them and know more about their lives.

5. Heaslop is upset and begins to question Mrs. Moore. He worries that Miss Quested may not understand the unwritten rules of behavior that would forbid such contacts between Indians and the English.

6. The word *"sahib"* identifies Heaslop as one who accepts his role in the Anglo-Indian governing class, displays class and ethnic solidarity, and can be counted on to maintain acceptable opinions and behavior.

7. This party is one to which Indians of a certain rank are invited in order to bridge the gap between them and the Anglo-Indians.

8. They believe the "natives" will not respect them anymore if they are able to meet socially. They pride themselves on hardly ever speaking to Indians.

9. Fielding believes that in order to know the real India, it is necessary to meet the actual Indian inhabitants. This causes him to be regarded as "not *pukka*."

10. The Major treats him like a subordinate, frequently summons him after hours, causes him to leave pleasant social occasions, and then keeps him waiting on the verandah or does not turn up at all.

Suggested Essay Topics

1. Compare and contrast the ways in which social cohesiveness is maintained among the Muslims and the Anglo-Indians. Include a description of their social habits, attitudes, and opinions.

2. Discuss the phenomenon of the outsider. Who are the actual and potential outsiders in the novel? In what way are the Muslims and the English outsiders to each other?

Chapters IV – VI

New Characters:

Nawab Bahadur: *wealthy Muslim landowner*

Mr. Ram Chand: *Hindu associate of Dr. Panna Lal*

Mr. Graysford and Mr. Sorley: *Anglo-Indian missionaries*

Miss Nancy Derek: *Anglo-Indian companion to a Maharani*

The McBrydes: *Anglo-Indian District Superintendent of Police and his wife*

Mr. and Mrs. Bhattacharya: *Hindus of some wealth and status*

Mrs. Das: *a relation*

Dr. Panna Lal: *Hindu doctor, Aziz's fellow assistant*

A subaltern: *Anglo-Indian army officer of lower rank*

Summary

Some of the Muslims discuss whether or not they should accept Turton's invitation to the gardens of the Club. The Nawab Bahadur believes that they should go, and his influence prevails. The narrator refers to all of those Indians who are so poor and considered so insignificant that they have not been invited, and to the missionaries Mr. Graysford and Mr. Sorley, who minister to this stratum of society and never come to the Club.

Chapter V takes us to the bridge-party. Heaslop and Mrs. Turton are condescending to the Indian women, who are uneasy and uncertain about how to behave. Mrs. Moore and Miss Quested try to open a conversation with them. Mrs. Moore asks if they may visit Mrs. Battacharya and Mrs. Das in return. Mr. Turton is perfunctory in his greetings. Only Mr. Fielding comes in and talks to everyone. Speaking to Miss Quested afterwards, he invites her and Mrs. Moore to tea. Adela is angry and miserable at the way the Indians have been treated.

Later, Mrs. Moore and her son, Ronny Heaslop, talk. Heaslop speaks of the difficulties he encounters as a magistrate. Mother and son disagree about the way the English should behave in India. The question of whether Heaslop and Miss Quested will marry is on Mrs. Moore's mind.

The first scene of Chapter VI takes place earlier in time, before the party. Aziz is shown at his work as a surgeon. Major Callendar scolds him for not having arrived in time at the bungalow the previous night. Aziz thinks of his wife and her death and is saddened. He receives a note from Fielding inviting him to tea and is overjoyed. Instead of going to the party in the Club gardens, he

goes to the *maidan* and plays polo with an unidentified subaltern. Later, in the presence of the Hindu Dr. Panna Lal, Aziz hits a Brahminy bull with his polo mallet.

Analysis

In this section Forster quietly introduces the idea of the Spirit of India. It is this spirit that Miss Quested and Mrs. Moore sense, without comprehending it. The spirit is beyond forms of government or codes of social behavior. It can be seen as the essence of the country.

A sensitivity to the Spirit of India is indicated by an interest in meeting and mixing with Indians. This interest, shared by Fielding, Miss Quested, and Mrs. Moore, is in itself enough to marginalize them in Anglo-Indian society. Fielding's status as an outsider is emphasized when he says he seldom goes to the Club. Miss Quested's sense that she too is an outsider, leads her to think in terms of allies. This introduces a theme that will define the sometimes shifting alliances that they and other characters form in the course of the book. Within the main groupings there are the subgroups of Hindu and Muslim, and *pukka* and non-*pukka* Anglo-Indians. Within those large groups, there are alliances that depend on individual qualities and on social attitudes.

The "bridge-party" takes place, and raises the question of how and to what degree the gulf between different cultures can be bridged. There are differing social codes that cause misunderstandings between members of the different groups. Mrs. Moore's idea of visiting the Indian women gives them pleasure, but there is a certain confusion about the timing and a sense of miscommunication. There is also miscommunication between Dr. Panna Lal and Aziz. Aziz and the Anglo-Indian subaltern succeed in bridging the gap between the races during their polo match, but the glow rapidly fades when it is over.

This section begins to penetrate more deeply into the private thoughts and feelings that lie behind the facade that people maintain to control others or protect themselves. There is a contrast between what people are outwardly saying and doing and what they are actually thinking and feeling. Adela Quested is silently preoccupied by visions of what her life will be like if she marries

Heaslop. And although Heaslop seems outwardly like the model of brutish conformity, his conversation with his mother reveals that he has inner conflicts, and a desire to do good in India. Still, his mother detects the lack of a "true regret from the heart." This suggests that Heaslop will continue to be dominated by the need to keep up appearances.

Aziz's character is further developed. His innermost feelings center around memories of his dead wife, yet he soon forgets her and is in the mood for a game of polo. He is impulsive, yielding to the unfortunate desire to make an enemy of Dr. Panna Lal by galloping his pony and causing the Hindu's pony to bolt, a scene that also strikes the note of latent enmity between Hindus and Muslims. These traits will later determine Aziz's behavior in the crisis that is the high point of the plot.

The word "god" and the question of religion enter this section. The missionaries, Mr. Sorley and Mr. Graysford, are mentioned. They are perhaps the ultimate outsiders, ministering to the Indians and playing no part in Anglo-Indian social life. Their doors are open to all, regardless of race. This might seem admirable, but Forster belittles them by including a farcical discussion on the acceptability of monkeys, jackals, and wasps.

The tone deepens during Mrs. Moore's conversation with her son. She begins by accusing the Anglo-Indians of posing as gods. These little gods are implicitly criticized as she goes on to speak of God's purposes for India. She is aware of her son's dislike of this theme. Like much else in Heaslop, his religion is limited to outward observance; he regards his mother's references to God as a sign of ill health. However, Mrs. Moore has found herself constantly thinking of God since she arrived in India. This God is love, she says hesitantly, and is omnipresent. The difference is between an outer observance of Christianity and an approach to a deeper sense of it. The chapter ends with the suggestion of an emptiness beyond even God, something beyond the remotest echo.

Study Questions

1. Why do the other Indians allow Nawab Bahadur to convince them to go to the party?

2. What information does Mrs. Turton give Mrs. Moore about the rank of Englishwomen in India in relation to Indian women?

3. Why does Mrs. Turton know only the imperative forms of Urdu?

4. What does Heaslop believe is the purpose of the English in India?

5. What does Mrs. Moore believe their purpose is?

6. Why doesn't Aziz go to the party?

7. What proves Major Callendar's ignorance of Indian life?

8. Why is it offensive to Dr. Panna Lal when Aziz hits the Brahminy bull with his polo mallet?

9. In what ways are Aziz and Heaslop similar in their attitudes toward work?

10. What are Aziz's feelings as he gazes at the photograph of his dead wife?

Answers

1. As a wealthy landowner, the Nawab has more prestige than the others and is considered a leader.

2. Mrs. Turton tells Mrs. Moore that she—and by implication, any Englishwoman—is superior in rank to any Indian woman except one or two of the *Ranis*, who are equal in rank to the Anglo-Indians.

3. Mrs. Turton is accustomed to speaking the language only to servants and has never bothered to study it for any other purpose.

4. He feels the English are in India to do justice and keep the peace. He believes he is in India "to work and hold this wretched country by force."

5.   Mrs. Moore believes the English "are in India to be pleasant." As God has put people on earth for the same purpose.

6.   It is the anniversary of his wife's death and he is saddened by his reverie about her. He is afraid the Anglo-Indian women will make fun of his sorrow.

7.   When Major Callendar begins to rebuke Aziz for not arriving on time the previous week, the Major cannot understand why Aziz's bicycle should have broken down in front of the Cow Hospital. It doesn't occur to him that instead of being at home, Aziz might have been visiting friends, and that this activity indicates the weaving of a new social fabric among the Indians.

8.   The Brahminy bull, and cows in general, are held sacred by the Hindus.

9.   They both work hard and are often not recognized or rewarded for it, Heaslop by the Indians, Aziz by the Anglo-Indians.

10. Tears flow from Aziz's eyes as he gazes at his wife's photograph. He feels self-pity as well, and attempts unsuccessfully to remember his wife.

Suggested Essay Topics

1.   Religion can be either a matter of outward observance or deep inward feeling. Contrast the religious beliefs of Mr. Sorley and Mr. Graysford, Ronny Heaslop, Aziz, and Mrs. Moore.

2.   Exclusion is a social mechanism that maintains the cohesiveness of a social group. Discuss ways in which exclusion is promoted in *A Passage to India*. Which characters attempt to work toward inclusion rather than exclusion? Give your opinion on whether exclusion is always undesirable or whether it is sometimes necessary.

Chapter VII

New Character:

Professor Narayan Godbole: *an elderly Hindu of the Brahmin caste*

Summary

Aziz is the first to arrive at Fielding's tea party. When Fielding can't find his collar stud, Aziz removes his and loans it to him. Mrs. Moore and Miss Quested arrive. Professor Godbole arrives and has his tea apart from the others. Aziz asks Miss Quested why she doesn't settle in India. Miss Quested replies that she couldn't do that, and is then surprised and taken aback at her reply. Aziz invites the party to visit the Marabar Caves with him. He has never been there; Professor Godbole describes them vaguely.

Ronny Heaslop arrives and wants to take Adela to see a polo game. He ignores Aziz and Professor Godbole, criticizes Fielding for leaving Miss Quested alone with Aziz and Professor Godbole, and makes disparaging remarks about Aziz. Aziz mentions that Miss Quested will not stay in India. They all say good-bye, feeling uneasy. As Heaslop, Miss Quested, and Mrs. Moore start to leave, Professor Godbole begins to sing a religious song to Shri Krishna. The chapter ends in silence.

Analysis

This chapter depends on rapid alterations of tone and mood, like a piece of music. It ends with a musical composition, a song that is unfamiliar to European ears. Although some outward forms of civility are maintained, the mood shifts rapidly throughout the chapter.

It begins with a growing intimacy between Aziz and Fielding. This provides further development of both these characters. Fielding treats Aziz with easy informality. Aziz is pleased to find that Fielding's home does not fit the Muslim's stereotype of English order, "everything ranged so coldly on the shelves." Privately, he thinks of the English as "cold and odd and circulating like an ice stream." This emphasis on cold is in contrast to his own warm

nature. He is excitable and changeable, carried away by his impulsiveness. When Aziz offers Fielding his own collar stud, he demonstrates his generosity. However, his uncontrollable chatter and his use of English slang make him seem faintly ridiculous.

The keynote to this chapter, and to much of the novel, is revealed in Mrs. Moore's remark about muddle and mystery. These terms serve to describe most of the social intercourse at Fielding's party. Even the first scene between Fielding and Aziz contains false notes.

Muddles are easy to spot. The greatest of them, the pivotal event upon which the unfolding of the entire novel rests, is Aziz's invitation to the Marabar Caves. Forster's irony is evident; Aziz invites the women only in order to distract them from the possibility of coming to his house. He has never been to the caves and knows nothing about them.

While Professor Godbole offers to describe them, the description consists mostly of negatives. No one seems to know why they are of any interest at all.

Although the members of different groups are face-to-face and in conversation at this tea party, there are still layers within a culture that outsiders find very difficult to penetrate. This is illustrated by the conversation between Aziz and Professor Godbole about the caves. Realizing that Professor Godbole is concealing information about the caves, and attempting to lead him into revealing more, Aziz begins to play a sort of mental game with him. The narrator informs us that Miss Quested is entirely unaware of the underdrift of this conversation, even though the talk goes on for some time.

The most extreme shift in mood occurs when Heaslop enters. He is annoyed to find Miss Quested alone with two Indian men and addresses himself only to her, ignoring Aziz and Professor Godbole. Oblivious to his own rudeness, Heaslop later remarks that he couldn't have upset the Indians because he hadn't even spoken to them. Forster's irony underscores this example of the Anglo-Indian refusal to recognize that their Indian subjects have human feelings.

The mood of general irritation ushered in by Heaslop shifts entirely once again, this time due to Professor Godbole's song, a song full of yearning for the absent Beloved, the mystery of the absent God. His song reveals another side of Professor Godbole. Although he has previously seemed only polite and enigmatic, he now appears in the character of a spiritual devotee. The song that he sings is a revelation of the Spirit of India, which dedicates itself to the worship of the invisible presence that is behind and beyond all forms. It affects the listeners deeply, and its consequences reach far beyond the scene in which it is sung.

Study Questions

1. Why does Aziz go biking in English dress rather than a *fez?*
2. Why is Aziz offended by Fielding's response to his remark about Post-Impressionism?
3. What is Fielding's definition of the difference between a mystery and a muddle?
4. Why does Aziz invite the party to the Marabar Caves?
5. Why does Heaslop tell Fielding he shouldn't have left Miss Quested alone with Aziz and Professor Godbole?
6. What is Aziz's description of Deccani Brahmins?
7. What does Professor Godbole say about the Marabar Caves?
8. Why does Miss Quested feel she should have told Heaslop about her decision not to settle in India before telling the others?
9. Why is everyone irritable as they say good-bye?
10. Does Shri Krishna answer the yearning call of the milk-maidens in Professor Godbole's song or in any other one?

Answers

1. Aziz has discovered that he is often stopped by the police if he is wearing native dress, in this case, a *fez.*
2. Aziz believes—wrongly—that Fielding is implying that a native could know nothing about such topics as Post-Impressionism.
3. Fielding believes that a mystery is "only a high-sounding term for a muddle."
4. Aziz is horrified at the thought of the others seeing his miserable one-room shanty. He invites them to the caves in order to distract them and to provide another setting.

5. In the view of Anglo-Indians, native men constitute a threat to Englishwomen, and it is the duty of an Englishman to chaperone Miss Quested.

6. He believes they have a very high opinion of themselves. They are also subtle, extremely rich, and have a great deal of influence.

7. Professor Godbole is vague in his description of the caves. He says there is an entrance in the rock, that there are no sculptures in them, and that they are not ornamented in any way.

8. Since Miss Quested may become engaged to Heaslop, her decision not to stay in India means she will not marry him. She feels this is a private decision, and strangers have no right to hear it first.

9. Mrs. Moore has been disturbed by Adela's announcement that she will not stay in India. Heaslop's arrival and his snubbing of Aziz and Professor Godbole has upset everyone except the Brahmin himself. Aziz has chattered tactlessly; Heaslop has irritated Fielding by criticizing him and irritated Mrs. Moore and Miss Quested by his rudeness. Only Professor Godbole is inundated with tranquility.

10. No, according to Professor Godbole, Shri Krishna does not arrive, in this or any other devotional song.

Suggested Essay Topics

1. Do you think Fielding's party was a success or a failure? Support your argument with examples.

2. Harmony is a quality not often depicted in *A Passage to India*. Professor Godbole seems to embody it. What are the signs by which we can tell that the Professor leads a harmonious life?

Chapter VIII

New Characters:

Mr. Harris: *the Eurasian chauffeur*

Krishna: *an attendant in Heaslop's office*

Nureddin: *the Nawab's grandson*

Summary

After leaving the party, Ronny Heaslop picks out Aziz's missing collar stud as a clue to the forgetful character of all Indians. Mrs. Moore does not want to go to the polo game, and Adela also declines, so Heaslop decides to drop the polo. Losing his temper, he orders his mother and Adela to have nothing to do with Indians in the future. He and Adela leave Mrs. Moore at the bungalow and go to the polo game after all. While they are at the polo grounds, Adela requests a "thorough talk," and she says she will not marry him. They see a bird that no one seems able to describe.

The Nawab Bahadur arrives at the *maidan* and offers them a ride in his car. The Nawab gets into the front seat next to his chauffeur and falls asleep. Heaslop tells the chauffeur to take a different road. Suddenly, there is an accident and the car runs into a tree on the embankment. Miss Quested says that they hit an animal, which caused the car to go off the road, but no one seems to be able to determine what kind of animal it was.

Miss Derek drives by in "her" Maharani's car and picks up everyone but the chauffeur. Nawab Bahadur praises the orderliness of British India, contrasting it to the superstition of the Indians. Heaslop and Adela, who have grown closer during the ride, decide to marry after all. Heaslop apologizes for his remarks. After the Nawab leaves the car, they go back to the bungalow, and before they go in, Miss Quested retracts her earlier refusal to marry Heaslop. They go into the bungalow and announce their engagement.

Mrs. Moore begins to think about going back to England. When they tell her of the accident, she says: "A ghost!" Heaslop carries on about "the native." He begins to call to Krishna, the worker who was supposed to bring his files to the office, despite Heaslop's

shouting, he does not appear. Adela and Mrs. Moore play a game of Patience and discuss marriage and honesty.

Surrounded by several others, the Nawab Bahadur is waiting for his car. He remembers an incident nine years before in which he had driven over a drunken man and killed him. He also speaks of the accident that had just happened and how horrified he is at risking the lives of his guests. Aziz whispers to Nureddin that it is necessary for Muslims to rid themselves of superstitions.

Analysis

To the previous examples of muddle, mystery, and misunderstanding, this chapter adds misidentification. It is introduced when Adela notices a bird at the polo grounds. She asks Heaslop its name; he guesses wrong, and the bird remains just "some Indian wild bird." The narrator explicitly tells us that "Nothing in India is identifiable."

The climax of the chapter, the car accident, also involves a beast that cannot be identified. Adela believes that some dark and hairy animal caused the accident. Although the chauffeur locates the mark on the car, no one is sure if the animal was a goat, a hyena, or a buffalo; it is all conjecture.

Another kind of mystery surrounds this accident. When Mrs. Moore is told of it, she gasps, "A ghost!" This underlines Mrs. Moore's role in the novel. She is unconsciously aware of things, and thus stirs up buried truths without realizing it. She scarcely knows what she has said or why, but afterwards, we learn that the Nawab Bahadur once drove over a drunken man and killed him. Although he has made reparation in every way he can, he still finds that the man's spirit lies in wait for him. In his mind, that is what caused the accident. The Nawab's earlier criticism of superstition is shown to be superficial—that is, to the rational mind that does not believe in ghosts.

A lighter, more ironic muddle is contained in Heaslop's references to Aziz's missing collar stud, a motif that recurs in this chapter. Heaslop's use of the generic term "the native" has already indicated that he is unable to differentiate between one Indian and another. To him, the missing collar stud is an example of Indians' lack of attention to detail; they always let you down, he warns Adela.

As readers, we have seen Aziz lend his collar stud to Fielding and therefore understand that the missing collar stud is a sign of generosity, not negligence. Similarly, we are aware of the Nawab's deep concern about the accident, and possible injury to his guests, while Heaslop believes he was indifferent. This type of muddle, of course, is due to prejudice, not innocent confusion.

Another recurring motif is the idea of god and the name of Krishna. An insignificant worker in Heaslop's office bears the name of the Hindu deity. Heaslop shouts and bellows for him, in an unconscious parody of Professor Godbole's call to the god. In both cases, the result is the same. Krishna does not come.

Again, there are ominous foreshadowings. The accident itself occurs on the Marabar Road, hinting that the expedition to the caves may not be a happy one. Heaslop speaks of the coming festival of Mohurram, when Muslims mourn the martyrdom of Mohammed's sons. It has often been the occasion for Hindu/Muslim strife, and the Anglo-Indians are anticipating more trouble.

Study Questions

1. Why didn't Heaslop pay attention to Aziz's previous announcement that Miss Quested would not stay in India?

2. Why is Miss Quested ashamed of Heaslop's behavior at the tea party?

3. Why does the chauffeur take the Marabar Road rather than the Gangavati?

4. Why is Mr. Harris self-conscious when he is together with Indians and Anglo-Indians?

5. In what way is Miss Derek condescending to Heaslop?

6. What is Miss Quested's reaction to this condescension?

7. What is the Nawab Bahadur's mental picture of the Maharani? What is his opinion of superstition at this point?

8. Why does Miss Quested feel humiliated after she agrees to marry Heaslop?

9. What makes the Nawab Bahadur a "show Indian"?

10. Why is Heaslop concerned about the approach of the Mohurram festival?

Answers

1. It has never occurred to Heaslop that an Indian might convey something important between two English people.

2. She feels he has been gross and spoiled both the conversation and the song, the latter by walking away in the middle of it. She also dimly realizes that she is really irritated with herself and is taking it out on him.

3. Heaslop changes the instructions that the Nawab has given the chauffeur. He says that Gangavati Road is under repair. They end up on Marabar Road.

4. Mr. Harris is Eurasian and feels rejected by both races.

5. Miss Derek implies that Heaslop is of lower status, since he has no contact with the wealthy and titled Indians that she is employed by.

6. Miss Quested is annoyed by the condescension and feels protective of Heaslop.

7. The Nawab imagines the Maharani as uneducated and superstitious. He praises British reason and orderliness in contrast, and says that superstition must be eradicated in India.

8. She feels that she is now labeled and her life will be all too predictable.

9. He tends to agree with and praise the English rule and to help induce other Indians to fulfill the wishes of their rulers. Therefore, he can always be pointed to as an example of an Indian who helps the Anglo-Indians to sustain their fantasies about themselves.

10. Mohurram, a festival in which there is loud and emotional mourning for the martyred sons of Mohammed, is a time when Hindus and Muslims frequently find occasion for quarrels and fighting.

Suggested Essay Topics

1. Trace the theme of identification, or labeling, in this chapter. Give examples, and show the different contexts in which it occurs. How does Miss Quested feel about labeling? Heaslop? In your opinion, is labeling desirable or undesirable?

2. Heaslop uses the term "show Indian." Our term is "tokenism." In what ways is the Nawab Bahadur a token Indian? Explain.

Chapters IX – XI

New Characters:

Hassan: *Aziz's servant*

Syed Mohammed: *a Muslim engineer*

Mr. Haq: *the Muslim police inspector*

Rafi: *Syed Mohammed's nephew*

Summary

Aziz is ill in bed. He fantasizes about dancing girls and sex. Hamidullah, Syed Mohammed, Mr. Haq, and Rafi come to visit and sympathize. Rafi first suggests that Aziz and Professor Godbole must have become ill after having tea with Fielding, then maintains that Professor Godbole has cholera. Syed Mohammed and the others speak scornfully of Hindus as a source of infection. Dr. Panna Lal arrives, accompanied by Ram Chand. He examines Aziz perfunctorily. The others inquire about Professor Godbole's illness. The Hindus and Muslims begin to quarrel.

Fielding enters and there is friendly joking. The conversation turns to God; he says that he doesn't believe in God. He is asked: "How is England justified in holding India?" and has no real answer, saying that he, personally, is in India because he needed a job. The Indians are unable to understand what he means. There is a discussion about whether or not India is spiritual.

The focus is on the larger picture, in which human beings play only a minor role. The heat and the approach of bad weather are emphasized. The sun is depicted as powerful but sinister, finally, only a creature.

Although the rest of Aziz's visitors have left, no one has brought Fielding his horse. He stays, and Aziz tells him to unlock a drawer and look at the photograph of his late wife. Fielding is touched and flattered. Aziz says that India needs "kindness, kindness and more kindness."

They talk of women, marriage, and children. Aziz suggests that Fielding marry Miss Quested and Fielding replies that she is engaged to Mr. Heaslop. Referring to the previous conversation with the others, Aziz warns Fielding to be careful what he says. Fielding gets up to go and asks Aziz to tell the servant to bring his horse. Aziz reveals that he has previously told the man not to bring it. Aziz is left considering Fielding as rash, but happy in the thought that they are friends.

Analysis

This final section in Part I reiterates and develops themes that have previously appeared. Aziz's reverie on sex continues to indicate the practicality and relative unsentimentality of his attitude toward it. We have already learned sexual feeling played little part in his love for his dead wife. Now, he muses about going off to Calcutta and visiting the *nautch* girls.

The division, misunderstanding, and mistrust between groups is heightened now. Hamidullah says that he can't even trust his fellow Muslims Syed Mohammed and Haq; he calls Syed's nephew Rafi, a malicious inventor of rumors, a "scorpion." There is even greater division between Hindus and Muslims, who soon begin to trade personal insults. In the midst of these undercurrents, Fielding has remained candid and confiding; Aziz finds this unwise and warns him about spies and careless talk.

The possibility of brotherhood is heightened too, stretching across the gap between their respective groups, as Aziz invites Fielding to see the photo of his wife, saying: "All men are brothers." This act seals their friendship, yet Fielding is aware of his own incapacity for intimacy, with Aziz or anyone else. He posits a conflict between intimacy and clarity.

Again, mood and emotion fluctuate as both characters are fully developed. Aziz ranges from petty tricks (arranging to keep Fielding's horse away from him) to sublime poetry. For his part, Fielding is aware that his experiences seem drab beside the tragedy of the death of Aziz's wife, and that their friendship is limited by his own stunted emotions. Fielding and Aziz also differ in that the Englishman is comparatively rootless, traveling light, while Aziz's life is deeply rooted in family and society.

One of the interests that unites them is a love for poetry. When Aziz recites a poem by Ghalib, the discord between groups and individuals is stilled, transcended. The poem is compared to the song calling to Krishna, as a less explicit call that also voices "our loneliness, our isolation, our need for the Friend...." This Friend is, in Islamic terms, God the Beloved, the friend beyond all friends. However it is expressed, this spiritual aspiration is a basic human yearning. Yet once again the narrator's rationality intervenes to remind us that poetry also falsifies, precisely because it lends divided Chandrapore a sense of unity. He also tells us that, for Aziz, literature may arouse either spiritual or sexual longings.

A short chapter depicts the overwhelming experience of the heat, in which all share equally. The heat and the sun become presences, almost characters. They are far stronger than human beings, and Forster again emphasizes the fact that human life is insignificant to most other life forms on earth, and that only a few people are deeply concerned with human political arrangements. The annual Anglo-Indian exodus to the hills to escape from the heat becomes "a retreat on the part of humanity."

Study Questions

1. Why is Rafi called "the Sherlock Holmes of Chandrapore"? Is he an accurate detective?

2. How do Aziz's visitors react to the poem he recites?

3. Why does Fielding's remark about atheism lead the Indians to ask him why the English are justified in holding India?

4. What is the reply Fielding could have made and doesn't? Why not?

5. Why are the Indians unable to understand the terms in which Fielding is talking?

6. Why had Aziz ordered his servant not to bring Fielding's horse when the other visitors left?

7. What is the corollary that Aziz adds to his remark that all men are brothers?

8. On what grounds do the Hindus and Muslims begin to quarrel?

9. How does Fielding feel about intimacy?

10. Why does Aziz think that Fielding is unwise?

Answers

1. Rafi claims to know everyone's secrets, but most of the rumors he purveys turn out to be inaccurate.

2. Although Hamidullah is the only one beside Aziz who is a reader of poetry, the rest are touched by it; they appreciate its pathos and it voices their loneliness.

3. The Indians take it for granted that authority should be rooted in spiritual qualities. On hearing that most educated English people are atheists, they naturally question the grounds for English rule of "spiritual" India.

4. The standard British answer would be: "England holds India for her good." Fielding cannot in honesty say this, since he does not entirely believe it.

5. Fielding is talking in terms of chance and self-interest. The Indians are used to thinking in terms of justice and morality, and find it difficult to comprehend an argument that makes no reference to these values.

6. Aziz wanted to detain Fielding so they could have a conversation alone.

7. He says that all men are brothers when they behave as such.

8. They begin to insult each other and each other's relatives, seemingly out of latent hostility. No particular incident provokes these insults.

9. Fielding realizes he will not become an intimate friend of Aziz, or of anyone else. Then he reflects that this is all right with him.

10. Fielding's candid talk with a group of people he doesn't know very well seems reckless to Aziz, who warns that they might be inclined to harm him by reporting his words to others.

Suggested Essay Topics

1. Discuss the following pairs of opposites: wisdom and honesty; intimacy and clarity. Why does Aziz think the first pair are opposites? Why does Fielding believe the second pair are incompatible? Present your own view, with examples.

2. Trace the way in which rumors arise in the societies of Chandrapore, giving examples of similarities and differences between this process and the way rumors are transmitted in our society. Include your conclusions about the origins and effects of rumors.

Part II: Caves
Chapters XII – XIV

New Character:

Antony: *Mrs. Moore's and Miss Quested's servant*

Summary

The Marabar Hills, one of the oldest geographical phenomena in the world, stand at a border where newer lands are advancing to cover the old. The repetitive layout of the caves is easily described, but there is something extraordinary and inhuman, or extra-human, about them that escapes description. They are dark inside, yet if a visitor strikes a match an answering flame is mirrored on the exquisitely polished walls of the circular chamber.

From the upper verandah of the Club, the hills look distant and romantic. Here Miss Quested is overheard remarking that she would like to have visited the caves. This report, magnified by rumor, travels to Aziz and forces him to begin planning an expedition. He asks Fielding and Godbole, and requests Fielding to invite the women. Everyone accepts, although no one is enthusiastic about this picnic.

Aziz makes elaborate arrangements, including borrowing servants from his friends. Miss Quested, Mrs. Moore, and their servant arrive early in the morning, but Aziz persuades them to

leave their servant behind. Fielding and Godbole have been delayed by Godbole's *pujah*, and when the train starts up, they are still on the other side of the level crossing. Aziz jumps onto the footboard, and in response to his howls, Fielding attempts to jump on, but misses his friend's outstretched hand and falls back onto the line. Mrs. Moore reassures Aziz that the expedition has not been ruined, after all.

In the *purdah* carriage, Mrs. Moore and Miss Quested chat about Adela's forthcoming marriage. When they look out, the hills are still dark. Adela remarks that they must be near the place where her "hyena" was. She is thinking about her entry into Anglo-Indian life. An elephant is waiting to take the women to the caves. They climb up the ladder to the *howdah* as the train moves off.

Aziz insists on feeding his guests. He discourses on the Moghul Emperors Babur, Alamgir, and Akbar. Adela voices her fear of becoming like the other Anglo-Indians when she marries Heaslop.

They enter the cave, vanishing down a hole. Inside, Mrs. Moore nearly faints. She becomes separated from Aziz and Adela and is temporarily disoriented and maddened. The echo in the cave contributes to this. Though she conceals her true feelings from the others, when Aziz and Adela set off for the other caves, Mrs. Moore makes an excuse to stay behind. In their absence, she is invaded by feelings of despair.

Analysis

In this section, *A Passage to India* leads its readers deeper into territory that lies beyond the scope of a traditional bourgeois novel. The question of marriage is revealed as a subplot rather than a central issue. The central issue is the encounter between people raised in bourgeois England and a wild, primal country.

The technique of subordinating human characters to a larger backdrop is repeated in the first chapter of Part II. This time Forster evokes the ancient land of India, the one that has seen the Himalayas rise from the ocean and an adjoining continent sink into the sea. The Marabar Hills belong to the original, primal land of India and stand at the juncture between the ancient land and the newer one that is encroaching on it. This Nature symbolism informs us that the ancient and the modern are about to come into contact.

The symbol of the two flames occurs in the description of the caves. These two flames could be interpreted as the spirits of India and of England. They could also suggest physical and material reality, or the rational mind and the spiritual self. In any case, one is a beautiful reflection of the other. The overall theme of the novel, the longing for union and the impossibility of union, is depicted in this image.

We are approaching the indefinable caves. Adela is reminded of the car accident, where she first saw "her" hyena. On the way to the caves, she mistakes a stump of toddy-palm for a snake. The animal motif, and mistaken identity, underline the possibility of sinister misinterpretations. This is an ominous foreshadowing of a deeper mystery to come.

Spiritual journeys, we are reminded, are not always filled with joy and light. It is a sense of utter negation, when everything seems meaningless and hopeless, that overcomes Mrs. Moore in the caves. The spiritual pilgrim must pass through this stage of despair in order to reach ultimate truth.

For Mrs. Moore, it is the monotonous echo that undermines "her hold on life." The narrator describes it as overlapping into a howling that generates "a snake composed of small snakes." Since in Christian imagery, the snake is a symbol of Satan, this suggests the presence of evil. Yet evil does not consist of cruelty or depravity, but of the absence of all ethical values, the absence of even the possibility of values. Mrs. Moore has reached an outer limit where her Christianity cannot comfort her. Her senses are deranged.

After Mrs. Moore's experience in the caves, the echo is first mentioned. It will be referred to over again during the rest of the novel. The echo drives Mrs. Moore mad and continues to haunt Miss Quested. Like the caves themselves, it is described as monotonous and undistinguished, yet its power continues to resonate throughout the novel.

Study Questions

1. What do visitors usually feel about their experience of the Marabar Caves? Why do they find it difficult to discuss them?

2. What do the walls of the circular chamber look like when a match is lit inside?

3. What version of Miss Quested's remark in the Club reaches Aziz?

4. In what ways does Aziz rely on his friends' help to organize the expedition?

5. Why does Aziz suggest the women send their servant back? Why do they agree?

6. Why do Fielding and Godbole miss the train?

7. What is Mrs. Moore's opinion of marriage?

8. What mistake does Aziz make in overrating hospitality?

9. How does Aziz characterize the three Moghul Emperors he mentions, and why does he prefer Babur to Alamgir?

10. What causes Mrs. Moore to fall into a state of despair?

Answers

1. Visitors tend to be unsure whether or not they have had an interesting experience, or whether they have had an experience at all. It is the monotony of the caves, their lack of ornamentation, that makes them difficult to describe.

2. In the light of a match, the walls look like a mirror inlaid with beautiful colors.

3. According to the version that reaches Aziz, the ladies have been waiting for his invitation to the caves and are deeply offended because it has not arrived.

4. Aziz asks Fielding to invite the ladies for him, he borrows servants from his friends and cutlery from Mahmoud Ali. His greatest challenge is the elephant, which he manages by enlisting Hamidullah Begum to call on Nureddin's mother and asks her to ask Nureddin to approach the Nawab Bahadur about the elephant.

5. Aziz wants the servant gone because he is a Hindu; the ladies agree because he has acted snobbish and aloof.

6. Godbole delayed them by doing a *pujah*, or ceremony of religious worship.

7. She feels that marriage has been overrated, and that centuries of sexual relations have not brought people closer to understanding each other.

8. Aziz mistakes hospitality for intimacy and does not understand its inherent possessiveness.

9. Aziz says that Babur never abandoned hospitality and pleasure, and that he never betrayed a friend. The more pious Alamgir, he says, reserved his disapproval for Akbar, who attempted to embrace all of India with his new, syncretizing religion.

10. Terrified in the cave, Mrs. Moore has lost control. She begins to feel that the echo is destroying her values and the idea of value itself. As she sits alone, the incomprehensible vastness of the universe makes her Christian faith seem ridiculous.

Suggested Essay Topics

1. Describe Aziz's concept of hospitality and his hospitable behavior in this chapter. Forster tells us that hospitality is a capital virtue. He suggests it may also be a vice. Decide whether or not you agree and explain your reasons.

2. Analyze the character of Mrs. Moore as it is revealed in Chapter XIV. Are her reactions consistent with her behavior in previous chapters? If not, show how the change is indicated and explain why it happens.

Chapters XV – XVII

New Characters:

An Indian guide

Miss Derek's chauffeur

A Brahmin cook: *hired by Aziz for Godbole*

Summary

Miss Quested, Aziz, and a guide continue the expedition, which is described as slightly tedious. Aziz is preoccupied with thoughts of the breakfast menu, and Adela with her coming marriage. She is suddenly struck by the thought that she and her fiancé do not love each other, and is appalled. As they climb in the heat, she begins to question Aziz about his marriage. Aziz claims that his wife is alive. Then Adela naively asks him if he has more than one wife. Aziz is insulted by the question and plunges away into another cave to regain his composure. Adela goes off into a different one.

When Aziz returns to look for her, he scolds the guide for not keeping her in sight. He attempts to search the other caves, but becomes completely confused. He realizes that the noise of the car he had previously heard indicates that friends of Miss Quested's are there, and he catches a glimpse of her far down the gully. He finds her field glasses lying in an entrance tunnel, the strap broken. He scrambles down to find Mrs. Moore and is delighted to discover that Fielding has arrived.

Aziz remarks airily that Miss Quested has gone down to visit Miss Derek. As they go down to escort Miss Derek to the picnic, her chauffeur stops them to announce that Miss Derek is driving Miss Quested back to Chandrapore herself. Fielding is startled, as this indicates a sudden change of plans. He, Mrs. Moore, and Aziz offer various explanations of why the two women have departed so hastily. In response to Fielding's questions, Aziz begins to falsify his account of what happened in the caves.

They return to the train. When they pull into Chandrapore station Mr. Haq, the Inspector of Police, flings open the carriage door and announces that he is arresting Aziz. Fielding's efforts to intervene

are futile. Aziz attempts to get away, but Fielding pulls him back. He promises to "see him through." Aziz is led off to prison.

Fielding goes to see the collector, who tells him that Aziz has "insulted" Miss Quested in the caves. Fielding protests and defends Aziz. Back on the platform, one of Ronny Heaslop's *chuprassies* is beginning to loot the train carriages. Although half-insane with rage, the collector stops the looting. On the way home, he promises himself to take revenge on all the Indians.

Analysis

In three relatively short chapters, the turning point of the novel is achieved and the events that follow it are set in motion. Mystery continues to surround the central event. What really happened in the caves? We have the narrator's account; we hear Aziz's various confusing and contradictory stories; and Mr. Turton informs Fielding of Miss Quested's accusation. These versions are contradictory and incompatible. Fielding, and eventually, Miss Quested, will repeatedly consider and reconsider the question of what really happened.

Again, muddle, misinterpretation, and miscommunication are heightened, this time to the point of madness. A general breakdown of rationality begins. Herd behavior takes possession of the Anglo-Indians. Fielding observes this, and it is he who calls Miss Quested mad.

One way to unravel the mystery surrounding Miss Quested's accusation is to consider the role of unconscious motives and desires. Forster appreciated Freudian theory, although he stated that the exploration of the unconscious was "not so much in Freud as in the air." In *A Passage to India*, Forster himself creates characters that are driven by forces beyond rationality, particularly the sexual drives that Freud considered paramount.

Though it is difficult to assess their actual behavior, most middle-class Englishwomen before the First World War largely repressed any verbal acknowledgment of sex. Mrs. Moore and Miss Quested are no exceptions. We are told that Miss Quested's senses have been stirred by Heaslop's "animal magnetism." Given the society of the time and their value structure, it would have been impossible for them to engage in sex before marriage. In this situation, Miss Quested's aroused but still unsatisfied sexual desires could easily have been stimulated by her proximity to Aziz, who has been described as an attractive and sensual man.

In contrast, Forster has repeatedly stressed Miss Quested's unattractiveness. One possibility is that she was attracted to Aziz, but that to her he was so foreign that sexual attraction seemed unthinkable. Her repressed desires, then, projected themselves onto Aziz, so that she imagined what she in fact wanted to happen. Aziz has been depicted as uninterested in her. We know also that he has no inhibitions about talking, or acting consciously and rationally about his sexual needs and desires. Therefore, his character, as depicted in the novel, would be unlikely to attempt a sexual assault on Miss Quested.

At the end of the chapter, there are two foreshadowings. The first is Mr. Turton's sense that Fielding has betrayed his group, foreshadowing his rejection by the Anglo-Indians. The second, is Mr. Turton's sense of justice, which narrowly prevails over his primitive rage.

Study Questions

1. Why does Adela not want to break her engagement to Heaslop, even though she has realized that they don't love each other?

2. What train of thought leads her to ask Aziz how many wives he has? Why is Aziz shocked by it? Is she aware of his shock?

3. Why does Aziz strike the guide?

4. What is Aziz's reaction when he hears that Miss Quested and Miss Derek have driven back to Chandrapore?

5. What causes the awkwardness between Mrs. Moore and Fielding? How does Aziz feel about it?

6. Why does Aziz conceal the truth about what happened in the caves?

7. Why does Mrs. Moore feel apathetic and cynical?

8. Why is Fielding annoyed with Miss Derek and Miss Quested?

9. Why does Fielding prevent Aziz from escaping arrest?

10. What forms of madness does Fielding perceive after the arrest? Does he understand madness?

Answers

1. Miss Quested reflects that marriage does not seem to depend on love. There is also the probability that breaking the engagement would cause her social embarrassment.

2. Adela has been musing about love and marriage herself, so it is natural for her to ask Aziz if he is married. It occurs to her that Muslims may have more than one wife, she then asks Aziz how many he has. For Aziz, having more than one wife is an old-fashioned custom of which he, as a modern Muslim, is ashamed. Adela is unaware that she has offended him.

3. Aziz strikes the guide because he feels frightened and worried and chooses to blame him for not looking after Miss Quested.

4. He is relieved, assuming that they have obeyed the same kind of impulse that he has often followed.

5. Mrs. Moore is suffering from her experience of despair. Fielding is annoyed with himself and chooses to include Mrs. Moore in his self-blame. They do not know each other well and feel awkward at finding themselves together on account of an Indian.

6. Aziz has never been particularly interested in verbal truth to begin with. He is embarrassed for Miss Quested, and wants to protect her by concealing the fact that she asked him such an insensitive question. His natural inventiveness then carries him away into a pleasant embroidery of the original story.

7. Her fainting in the cave has changed Mrs. Moore permanently. Her whole vision of India has been altered.

8. He feels they have been rude to Aziz by accepting his hospitality and then leaving without even an explanation.

9. Fielding can foresee that if Aziz escapes, there will be a manhunt and his guilt will seem certain.

10. Madness has taken possession of the collector, who is raving about the insult Miss Quested has suffered and the way the good name of his district has been ruined. He is angry with Fielding for not joining the collective madness that has engulfed all the other Europeans in Chandrapore. Fielding says that Miss Quested must have been mad to accuse Aziz in the first place.

Suggested Essay Topics

1. Discuss the way in which people misinterpret each other's motives in this section. Can you think of explanations that would have helped to clarify the situation? Write a sample dialogue between Miss Quested and Aziz, and between Aziz and Fielding, that would have prevented Aziz's arrest.

2. Trace the ways in which people are blamed and attempt to share or avoid blame in this section. Include a discussion of self-blame and blaming others. How is blame related to guilt?

Chapters XVIII – XXI

New Characters:

A young mother: *blonde Englishwoman, symbolizes British womanhood*

A subaltern: *British army officer of lower rank, supports Major Callendar*

Mr. Amritrao: *an Oxford educated, Hindu Calcutta barrister, notoriously anti-British*

Summary

Mr. McBryde detains Aziz, explaining that he may be released on bail. When Fielding arrives, McBryde explains the charge to him. Fielding asks to see Miss Quested, but his request is denied. He declares that he believes Aziz is innocent. His request to see Aziz is also denied. The contents of Aziz's table-drawer are brought in; Mr. McBryde says triumphantly, "Photographs of women." Fielding explains that the photograph is of Aziz's wife.

Hamidullah is waiting outside the superintendent's office. He prattles to Fielding about policy and evidence. Concentrating wholly on Aziz's innocence, he is aware of how his reactions differ from those of the Indians with whom he has decided to side. Hamidullah wants to hire Amritrao, a noted Calcutta barrister, to defend Aziz. He believes having a Hindu in charge of the defense will widen its appeal. Fielding next has a vague talk with Godbole. The professor talks of other matters and seems unconcerned about Aziz. He says he is to start a high school in Central India, in the state of Mau. Fielding begs him for a personal opinion on Aziz's innocence or guilt. Godbole dissolves the question into an abstract discussion of good and evil.

Fielding obtains a permit to see Aziz, who is miserable and unapproachable, charging the Englishman with having deserted him. Without much hope, Fielding writes a letter to Miss Quested.

Suddenly feeling that Miss Quested is one of them, the Anglo-Indian women discover a new affection for her. At the Club, a beautiful, young mother is transformed into a symbol of "everything worth fighting and dying for." The collector takes charge, giving instructions and telling the women that Aziz has been refused bail. Mr. Turton concludes by appealing to the Anglo-Indians not to suspect all Indians just because one has been charged with a crime.

Major Callendar enters; he feels responsible for having given Aziz leave. He uses the subaltern to bait Fielding. Then the Major, who is quite drunk, repeats a series of wild rumors about the way in which Aziz plotted the crime.

Ronny Heaslop enters. Fielding refuses to rise to his feet with the rest. The collector asks why he has refused to stand up. Taking this as the attack that it is, Fielding rises and announces that he believes Aziz is innocent. He resigns from the Club. Mr. Turton, enraged, begins insulting him. His way out is blocked by the subaltern, but Heaslop appeals to him to allow Fielding to go. On the upper verandah, Fielding is invaded by self-doubt and self-questioning.

Mohurram is in the air; drums are beating. The campaign to save Aziz is also heating up. Fielding spends the rest of the evening with Aziz's friends and defenders. They have received word that Amritrao has agreed to conduct the defense. Now that Miss Quested has been pronounced out of danger, they decide to renew application for bail. Later, Fielding would like to speak to Godbole about his mistake in being rude to Heaslop at the Club, but the professor has slipped away.

Analysis

The breakdown into herd behavior is almost the opposite of the breakdown that Mrs. Moore suffers in the caves. She is overcome by a sense of the meaningless of all values. The Anglo-Indians are swept away by emotions that assert the absolute primacy of certain collective values. Raw passions that are usually held in control by civilization are reasserting themselves. Fielding continues to be an observer, although he is aware of the danger of becoming caught up in the herd instinct and acts to avoid this.

A musical background is provided by the sound of the drums of Mohurram, which function as a reminder of impending trouble. Mohurram is a festival in which individuality is swallowed up within collective lamentation. Ironically, the Anglo-Indians, who are apprehensive about the riots that may be inspired by the festival, are also experiencing a loss of individuality in collective emotion. Even Anglo-Indians who are ordinarily quite different from each other begin to share the same emotions and reactions. Some of them acquire a symbolic value that overrides their individuality. In this way, Miss Quested, who has previously been barely tolerated as an outsider, becomes "one of us." The same mechanism turns a young mother everyone has ignored before into a symbol of English values. Heaslop, too, becomes a symbol of innocent suffering.

Two phenomena that are familiar to us appear: social bullying and power politics. Under the cover of his drunkenness, Major Callendar attempts to bully Fielding. When the subaltern becomes Callendar's willing instrument, the bullying stops just short of a physical attack.

Power politics are undisguised. Fielding is a lone individual against a powerful group. The whole Club turns against him, defining him as a traitor, an enemy, an outsider. The English ideals of justice and fairness are threatened, though not entirely forgotten. Even though Fielding has insulted Heaslop, at this critical moment Heaslop tells the subaltern to let him go.

Social cohesiveness has become paramount for both the Anglo-Indians and the Indians. Just like the Hindus and Muslims after the shootings at Amritsar in 1919, the Hindu and Muslim characters in the novel are beginning to cooperate. There is a newborn Indian desire to bring all Indians together to defend Aziz. His friends gather around him. Fielding is the only Anglo-Indian among them. He will help in Aziz's defense, yet he is aware of how his attitudes and methods differ from those of the Indians. Although he has allied himself with the Indians, he is an outsider among them, as well.

For Fielding, the central issue is Aziz's innocence. He is saddened by Hamidullah's emphasis on policy and evidence. When Fielding attempts to talk to Professor Godbole about the case, the professor talks in abstractions, stating that Good and Evil are both aspects of the Lord, and consist essentially of the presence or absence of God. We all share equally in guilt or innocence, he says. Later on, when Fielding wants to consult him about a matter of conscience—his failure to stand when Heaslop entered the Club— the professor has slipped away. The values Western civilization is based on look very different to the Indians.

Study Questions

1. Why is Fielding's first request to see Aziz denied?

2. Why is Mr. McBryde triumphant when he finds a picture of a woman among the contents of Aziz's drawer?

3. What change has occurred in the Anglo-Indian women's feelings toward Miss Quested?

4. What are Mr. Turton's emotions as he speaks to the Anglo-Indians at the Club? Is he entirely ruled by his emotions at this time?

5. Why does Major Callendar feel guilty? How does he deal with his guilt?

6. What rumors does Major Callendar relay about Aziz? Are these rumors generally believed?

7. Why does Callendar's first attack on Fielding fail to mature?

8. Why do the Anglo-Indians rise to their feet when Heaslop enters? Why doesn't Fielding rise with the others?

9. Why does Fielding resign from the Club? Why does Mr. Turton call him weak?

10. Why does Fielding classify his rudeness to Heaslop as a tactical and moral error?

Answers

1. Fielding has revealed that the collector is against him, so McBryde feels both justified and supported in denying the request. McBryde also feels strongly that Anglo-Indians must stick together. In his eyes, by maintaining Aziz's innocence, Fielding is acting like a traitor.

2. The case McBryde is building against Aziz in his mind involves a picture of someone who is obsessed with sex. He's already found a letter from Aziz to a brothel-keeper; he assumes the picture must be of a prostitute.

3. Miss Quested, who has been regarded as an awkward outsider, now arouses all their protective feelings, along with a certain amount of guilt about their earlier treatment of her.

4. Mr. Turton is raging with pity and heroism. Officially he speaks to the British sense of fairness when he urges the others not to convict all Indians because one has been charged with a crime. We know Mr. Turton's thoughts; he is consumed with a desire for revenge on all Indians.

5. Major Callendar says that he contributed to the alleged attack by granting Aziz leave. His sense of guilt inspires outbursts of emotion in which he wants the army called up. He finds a way out by scapegoating Fielding, transferring his own guilt onto someone else.

6. The Major reports that Aziz bribed Godbole to make Fielding miss the train. He also says that Aziz paid natives to suffocate Mrs. Moore in the cave. Although Callendar's drunken and hysterical cries for calling up the army are discounted, his version of Aziz's premeditation seems to be generally believed.

7. Mr. Turton, who is the controlling figure at the Club, fails to support Callendar's attack.

8. They rise to honor him and to assure him of their support. Fielding is afraid that he will be carried along in solidarity with the rest if he does not make his position clear.

9. Fielding resigns from the Club as a sign that he is taking Aziz's side in this matter. Major Callendar calls Fielding weak because he refused to stand up with the other Anglo-Indians.

10. It is suggested that by refusing to stand, Fielding has insulted Heaslop. His intention was to make his own position clear. The tactical error may lie in his losing all hope of influence with the Anglo-Indians.

Suggested Essay Topics

1. Write an essay in which you explore the dangers of herd mentality. Include examples from the novel and also from history or contemporary life.

2. To Major Callendar's mentality, Fielding is a weakling. Explain why the Major thinks as he does. Is Fielding's action in resigning from the Club weakness or courage? Explain.

Chapters XXII – XXIII

New Character:

Lady Mellanby: *wife of the lieutenant-governor of the province*

Summary

Adela is recuperating in the McBryde's bungalow, with Miss Derek and Mrs. McBryde hovering over her, picking cactus spines from her flesh. Whenever she tells the story of the Marabar Caves, she begins to cry. Adela is plagued by a recurring echo that makes her feel that Evil has gotten loose and is entering other people's lives.

When Adela's temperature has fallen to normal, Heaslop takes her away. He tells her that there had nearly been a riot on the last day of Mohurram; the procession had tried to enter the civil station. When she learns that she will have to appear in court to identify Aziz and be cross-examined by an Indian lawyer, she asks to have Mrs. Moore with her.

Like other Anglo-Indians, McBryde and Heaslop are indignant that an Indian judge, even Ronny Heaslop's assistant, will preside over a case involving an Englishwoman. McBryde gives Adela a letter from Fielding. The superintendent tells her of Fielding's behavior at the Club and that he is now a mainstay of the defense. According to the superintendent, he is also responsible for the Mohurram troubles. Miss Quested reads the words, "Aziz is innocent." Her only response is to worry about Fielding's treatment of Heaslop.

As they near Mrs. Moore's bungalow, Ronny warns her not to expect too much; his mother is old and irritable, he says. Mrs. Moore greets her indifferently. She seems resentful and disinclined to help. Adela speaks of the recurring echo. Mrs. Moore says she has nothing to say. She refuses to testify. Each time Adela extends her hand, Mrs. Moore withdraws hers. She seems to focus entirely on her own concerns.

Suddenly Adela repeats, "Aziz, Aziz." She tells Heaslop Aziz is innocent, that she has made a mistake. Ronny attempts to distract her, telling her that Nureddin had stolen the Nawab's car during the riots and driven Aziz into a ditch. As a result, Aziz had been returned to prison. He calls Major Callendar to come examine Adela.

Returning, he finds that Adela is convinced she heard Mrs. Moore say that Aziz is good. Heaslop denies this, saying she is confusing this with Fielding's letter. Adela agrees. Ronny asks her not to speak of Aziz's innocence again. When questioned, Mrs. Moore replies that she had not said Aziz's name, but adds, "Of course he is innocent."

She calls herself a bad old woman, but still refuses to help them to wrongly convict Aziz. Confused, Adela vacillates. She asks if the case can be withdrawn, then says that she knows this is impossible. Heaslop concurs, saying the machinery has already started. Mrs. Moore says ominously, "She has started the machinery; it will work to its end." Heaslop's silent response is to plan to send his mother away from India as soon as possible.

Lady Mellanby, the lieutenant-governor's wife, offers to share her reserved cabin with Mrs. Moore. Mrs. Moore leaves as she had wished. She is living "in the twilight of the double vision," which is a state of "spiritual muddledom" that creates paralysis. Instead of uplifting her, her vision in the caves has revealed a maggoty eternity.

She travels alone on the train to Bombay and watches the passing landscape, thinking that she has not seen the right places in India.

Analysis

Following the climactic event of the trial, the theme of departure begins to assert itself. With the departure of Mrs. Moore, the character who has precipitated some of the main events in the novel disappears from the scene. Yet, while Mrs. Moore has served as a catalyst for other events, her active role is already over. Early in the novel, she held a fateful conversation with Aziz in the courtyard of the mosque. Later, her eagerness to meet Indians led to further developments. However, her experience in the Marabar Hills transforms her. From now on, Mrs. Moore begins to resemble a hollow, mysterious center, like the caves themselves. Her character exists as a passive space that continues to influence others without participating in action.

The echo Mrs. Moore first heard in the caves is now resounding in Miss Quested's ear. She too identifies it with Evil. She also relies on Mrs. Moore to free her from it. However, when Heaslop takes her to see the older woman, there is no help, only the ominous assertion that Miss Quested will continue to hear the echo from now on. Adela finds that her friend has withdrawn into a combination of petty personal concerns and a kind of babble. Here, Forster is depicting the state of mind of someone who has suffered a shock and has had a breakdown because of it. The effect of shock on Miss Quested is to make her childishly dependent; Mrs. Moore's transformation is more complete. Her words are rambling, though at times startlingly acute.

In Mrs. Moore, the breakdown takes the form of a withdrawal from human life. Formerly, she was eager for experience. Now she is preoccupied with "departure" in two senses: taking a ship back to England, and withdrawing from ordinary human responsibilities and concerns. She refuses to participate even in an event that deeply touches her, her friend, and her son. What might have become a spiritual revelation leading to true detachment has instead inspired a revulsion from life. When she speaks of retiring to a cave, it is a bitter, not a hopeful, vision.

Mrs. Moore's seemingly aimless, querulous chatter contains moments of surpassing clarity. At last she says—referring to Aziz: "It isn't the sort of thing he would do." She is also prescient in saying of Adela: "She has started the machinery; it will work to the end."

Curiously, even before Mrs. Moore has off-handedly affirmed Aziz's innocence, Adela believes she has heard her say: "Aziz is innocent." Considered rationally, this indicates that Miss Quested has made a mistake, one of the many muddles that have plagued her. Considered from the standpoint of telepathic communication, it indicates that she has picked up Mrs. Moore's belief before it has been stated aloud. From now on, Mrs. Moore's influence is to be transmitted subliminally, or spiritually.

Study Questions

1. Why does Miss Quested long to see Mrs. Moore?

2. What does her response to Fielding's letter suggest about her inner state?

3. What do Mrs. Moore's words and actions indicate when Adela arrives at the bungalow?

4. What are Heaslop's unspoken opinions of his mother?

5. Why does Heaslop ask Miss Quested not to speak of Aziz's innocence again?

6. What does Mrs. Moore mean by saying, "There are different ways of evil, and I prefer mine to yours"? What is Mrs. Moore's way of evil?

7. Why does Mrs. Moore believe Aziz is innocent? What do Heaslop and Miss Quested think of her belief?

8. Why does Heaslop suddenly want to send his mother away from India?

9. Why does Lady Mellanby offer to let her share her private cabin?

10. What is the significance of Mrs. Moore's remark, "there are worse evils than love"?

Answers

1. Miss Quested feels that her friendship with Mrs. Moore is deep and real. No one else understands her.

2. Her distracted response to Fielding's letter indicates that she is not able to face the question of Aziz's guilt or innocence.

3. Mrs. Moore doesn't rise to greet her. She seems uninterested in Adela and indifferent to her plea for friendship. Her words are ominous rather than reassuring.

4. Heaslop believes that others do not know his mother as he knows her. They think that she is just a sweet, old lady, but he has seen other sides to her that are less attractive and less kind.

5. He says that all his servants are spies, and that such a remark would help Aziz's defense if it were overheard.

6. Mrs. Moore implies that the accusation against Aziz and his trial are evil actions committed in the name of justice. Her way of evil may be non-participation, the refusal to take sides.

7. She says it is a matter of character, and that both English people and Indians have spoken well of Aziz. It isn't something he would do, she believes.

8. Heaslop scornfully dismisses this as "feeble." However, Adela's doubts are increased. She cannot dismiss the idea that she might be wrong.

9. This is a gesture of Anglo-Indian solidarity. It is the only thing Lady Mellanby can do in response to the appeal from the ladies of Chandrapore.

10. Mrs. Moore is preoccupied with evil at this point. She believes that an attempted sexual assault, here interpreted as love, is a lesser evil than the vengefulness and hatred that has possessed the Anglo-Indians.

Suggested Essay Topics

1. Like Mrs. Moore, Miss Quested's character seems to have changed entirely. Describe the changes that have occurred in the two women and suggest why they might have occurred.

2. Discuss the question of evil as it is presented in these chapters. Differentiate between different types and degrees of evil. Do you agree with Mrs. Moore's insights about the nature of evil?

Chapter XXIV

New Characters:

The punkah-wallah: *a beautiful Untouchable who works the courthouse fan*

Mr. Das: *Hindu judge presiding over the trial, Heaslop's assistant*

Summary

Adela is now staying with the Turtons. Ronny continues to support her faithfully, yet she asks herself if she is capable of loving anyone. Fearing that she will break down under cross-examination, she tells the Turtons that her echo has come back.

There are signs of unrest on the way to the court, and they hear further reports about it. The Anglo-Indians tend to blame Fielding. Major Callendar issues another brutal tirade against these "buck niggers," during which he refers mockingly to the disfigured face of Nureddin, now in the hospital after the accident. Mrs. Turton chimes in, calling the men weak and saying that the Indians should be made to crawl.

The case is called. The first person Adela notices is the humblest, a strong and beautiful Untouchable who pulls the cord of the hanging fan. She is impressed by the *punkah-wallah's* aloofness.

McBryde opens the case for the prosecution. His manner implies that Aziz is guilty and the trial only a formality. Describing the prisoner as a man of loose life, he deploringly remarks that darker races are physically attracted by lighter races, but not the other way around. An Indian spectator asks, "Even when the lady is so uglier than the gentleman?" He is ejected from the courtroom.

Miss Derek comforts Miss Quested, who is upset by the comment. Major Callendar demands that she be seated on the platform. Her companions come up with her, leaving Fielding as the only European in the main body of the hall.

Looking timidly around the courtroom, Miss Quested notices Aziz and wonders if she could have made a mistake. Mahmoud Ali requests that Aziz, too be seated on the platform, and is snubbed by Mr. Das. Then Mr. Amritrao rises to object to the presence of so many extraneous Europeans on the platform. Mr. Das cringes, but requests everyone but Miss Quested to step down. Only Heaslop supports him in this; the others grumble but descend.

McBryde continues his speech, referring to Fielding, among others, as the "prisoner's dupes." He insists on charging Aziz with premeditation and concludes by calling him vicious and degenerate. Mahmoud Ali, in a fit of rage, accuses McBryde of smuggling Mrs. Moore out of the country so that she wouldn't testify in favor of Aziz. He calls the trial a farce and leaves the courtroom.

Outside, the Indians take up the chant of Esmiss Esmoor—their version of Mrs. Moore—repeating it like a mantra. Mr. Amritrao apologizes for Mahmoud Ali, but reiterates the charge that Mrs. Moore has been smuggled out of the country. Now it is time for Adela to give her evidence.

As she begins to tell the story of the expedition, she relives it. She answers McBryde smoothly until he asks a leading question implying that Aziz followed her into a cave she had first entered alone. She asks for time to reply, then falteringly admits that she is not sure. McBryde unsuccessfully attempts to make her agree. Finally, in a low voice, she says that she has made a mistake.

McBryde tries to recall her to the accusation she made on her deposition, but Mr. Das addresses Miss Quested directly. Sensing disaster, Major Callendar wants to stop the proceedings on medical grounds. Miss Quested holds firm and insists on withdrawing the charge. Mr. Das declares the prisoner released without prejudice. In the courtyard, pandemonium reigns; the English are protected by their servants; Aziz faints in Hamidullah's arms.

Analysis

The trial scene provides the dramatic climax of the novel. Like all trials, it has the structure of a confrontation between two opposite sides. The groups that have previously been talking behind each others' backs are now face-to-face. At first, the power of the British Raj seems undeniable. Even the Hindu judge, Mr. Das, who is Heaslop's assistant, is cowed by the rank and self-assurance of the Anglo-Indians.

There are dramatic confrontations: the advance of the Anglo-Indians onto the platform, Mahmoud Ali's sensational ravings and departure, Amritrao's request that those not involved in the case be asked to step down. At least part of the structure of justice holds, when Mr. Das requests them to do so and Heaslop backs him up. Still, when McBryde begins to lead Miss Quested through her testimony, Aziz's conviction seems inevitable.

All this changes when Miss Quested withdraws her accusation. Suddenly, she finds herself able to withstand the social pressure placed on her and to throw off her childish dependence. Once again, she is the direct and honest person of the earlier chapters. Fielding notices ahead of time that something is happening.

She understands that her public recantation is not enough; there will still be a need for confession and atonement. These are words that belong to religious language, not to the language of the law courts. They indicate that what has happened to her is in the nature of an epiphany, a sudden opening that lifts her awareness to a higher level. Before giving testimony, she has defined "coming through all right" in terms of keeping her spiritual dignity. In fact, this is what happens, although it occurs in a way she does not foresee at the time.

The most suggestive symbol in this chapter is seemingly irrelevant to the central business of the trial. Perhaps the humblest figure in the courtroom is the *punkah-wallah*, an Untouchable who pulls the cord on the hanging fan. He never speaks, but his presence incarnates the presence of a mass of people Forster has previously reminded us of: those who have no rank or standing but who represent the spirit of India. He is described, not coincidentally, as divinely beautiful, and his image presides over the chapter like a voiceless god. On another level, Miss Quested's acute awareness of the *punkah-wallah's* body both emphasizes her susceptibility to male beauty and suggests another association, between sexuality and spirituality.

The other presiding deity of the trial is Esmiss Esmoor. In her absence, Mrs. Moore has been transformed into a Hindu goddess and her name into a popular religious chant. It is the memory of her kindness that the Indians honor. They believe that she wanted to save Aziz and blame Heaslop for spiriting her away. There is only a small bit of truth in this belief. Still, it is enough for the Indians, who have begun to worship her much transformed memory. Their chanting floats into the courtroom. Once again, Forster supplies a musical or rhythmical background that alters the atmosphere of a scene.

It could be said that this chant replaces the evil echo and subconsciously reminds Adela of truth. Yet, the reasons for Miss Quested's recantation are more than psychological. The presence of something supernatural in the figure of the *punkah-wallah* and in the "magic" chanting of the masses outside pervades the atmosphere of the courtroom. Miss Quested calls it "queer," yet in the midst of the chanting she assures her friends that she feels better. She will come through all right, she says. Like Professor Godbole's song to Krishna, the chant affects even those who do not share the belief that it expresses, even those who are unaware of its effects.

Study Questions

1. What are the ominous signs of unrest that precede the trial?

2. Why is Miss Quested sure she will get her verdict?

3. What point does Miss Quested not want to tell the truth about?

4. Why does Heaslop support Mr. Das in asking the Europeans to step down?

5. Why does Mahmoud Ali leave the court?

6. How does Heaslop react to hearing his mother turned into a Hindu goddess?

7. When McBryde states that Miss Quested entered the cave alone and then Aziz followed her in, what reply does he expect? Why does he expect this answer?

8. Why does Mr. Das insist on addressing Miss Quested himself? Is this in keeping with his previous behavior?

9. Why does Major Callendar want to stop the proceedings?

10. What is Aziz's reaction to the verdict?

Answers

1. A stone thrown at the Turtons' car, a group of threatening students, strikes by Sweepers, and a hunger strike by Muslim women indicate that trouble is brewing.

2. She has been surrounded by Anglo-Indians who have assured her that anything else is unthinkable.

3. She intends to tell the truth; the difficulty is that, like Aziz earlier, she is determined not to admit to the conversation they had just before entering the caves. She is embarrassed at having blundered, and now speculates that the question about marriage may have inflamed him and led to the attack.

4. Heaslop is himself a magistrate and has a sense of fairness that leads him to applaud a correct decision.

5. Mahmoud Ali has been in a rage throughout the trial. Rather than withdraw his sensational charge, since he cannot prove it, he leaves.

6. He is revolted.

7. McBryde expects Miss Quested to agree. Only two hours before, she has signed a deposition testifying to this. He led her through the questions before the trial began.

8. Mr. McBryde does not want her to withdraw the charges, and is attempting to influence her to return to her original version. This is the only way for Mr. Das to hear what she has to say. He has previously been timid, but is now at ease and authoritative.

9. Major Callendar wants to avoid the acquittal of Aziz. By claiming that Miss Quested is ill, he may imply that she has suffered a nervous breakdown which invalidates her current testimony.

10. He faints in Hamidullah's arms.

Suggested Essay Topics

1. Decide whether or not you think the trial is a farce. Explain and support your position.

2. Give your opinion as to why Miss Quested changed her testimony at the crucial time. Fielding believes she has had a nervous breakdown. Are there other explanations? Are there clues that the change is coming?

Chapters XXV – XXVI

Summary

Miss Quested is carried out of the courtroom by a mass of Indians. A riot is beginning. She is rescued by Fielding, who takes her to his *victoria*, ignoring Aziz's call to him. Students, placing garlands around Fielding's neck, pick up the shafts and carry them through the main bazaar. Despite the ill-feeling against Miss Quested, more garlands are flung around her neck and Fielding's.

As the procession continues, Mahmoud Ali tries to incite attacks on the English; Nawab Bahadur attempts to calm the crowd; Hamidullah says there must be an orderly procession. Aziz again accuses Fielding of desertion. Mahmoud Ali starts a rumor that Nureddin has been tortured. Howling, the mob heads for the hospital.

Dr. Panna Lal averts disaster, first by clowning to appease the mob, then by producing Nureddin. The Nawab Bahadur gives a speech during which he announces he will give up his British title and be known as Mr. Zulfiqar. The crisis over, he asks Hamidullah to bring Fielding and Amritrao to his residence.

That evening, Miss Quested requests an interview with the reluctant Fielding. She tells him she had not been feeling well before the expedition to the caves. Fielding posits three or four possibilities to explain her behavior: that Aziz did attempt to assault her; that she accused him out of malice; or that she had a hallucination.

Miss Quested traces her "illness" back to Professor Godbole's song at the tea party. She agrees she could have had a hallucination in the caves. Fielding tells her that he believes McBryde exorcised her by asking a straightforward question. This leads to talk of

ghosts, Mrs. Moore, and the supernatural; they both affirm rationalism. She asks about Aziz's opinion of her; Fielding softens it.

Fielding goes on to suggest the fourth possibility: it might have been someone else. Miss Quested offers, "the guide," but seems to lose interest. Hamidullah arrives and, pointedly ignoring Adela, asks Fielding to come over for the victory celebration. Fielding tells Hamidullah that Miss Quested has been explaining her conduct. She admits her mistake, but Hamidullah is still furious. He has overheard their talk about the guide and says sardonically, "Of course some Indian is the culprit, we must never doubt that."

Hamidullah again invites Fielding to the Nawab Bahadur's residence; Miss Quested announces she will go to the Dak Bungalow. They argue about the plan until Hamidullah sees Heaslop arriving. Adela goes out on the verandah to see him. Inside, Fielding tells Hamidullah that Mrs. Moore is dead.

Miss Quested returns, having learned of Mrs. Moore's death from Heaslop. She asks Fielding if she can stay at the college during his absence. Heaslop comes in uncertain of where Miss Quested should go, and Fielding invites her to stay at the college. Hamidullah brutally reminds Heaslop of Mrs. Moore's death and the son's false claim in court that she had reached Aden.

Later, driving out to the Nawab's residence, Fielding is horrified to hear Amritrao tell Hamidullah that Miss Quested should pay 20,000 rupees as compensation.

Analysis

The plot is now past the point of dramatic climax and is winding down. Rumor continues to create its intended dissension, yet despite Mahmoud Ali's rumors, the riotous mob is calmed without bloodshed.

In terms of character development, there are two definite shifts in this section. One concerns Fielding and Miss Quested, who have been only acquaintances, then estranged by the trial, and now begin to know each other better. The other is the sudden prominence of Hamidullah, who has previously been a dignified presence in the background.

The question that runs through the novel now, is: What really happened? Fielding offers various possibilities, but Miss Quested loses interest in determining which might be true. Hamidullah's entrance, just as she agrees it might have been the guide or one of a gang of Pathans, confirms the Muslim's underlying suspicion of the English. Fielding is the one who advanced these Indians as suspects. Even though he has defended Aziz, he is still demonstrating his unconscious racism.

The changes that the trial has made in the feelings among Indians are emphasized by Hamidullah's attitude. In place of his earlier desire for friendship with the British, Hamidullah now feels a bitter resentment that leads him to speak sarcastically to Miss Quested. When she confesses her mistake to Hamidullah, he is unmoved. Unlike Fielding, who has begun to be impressed by Miss Quested's plain-spoken honesty, Hamidullah notes her absence of passionate feeling and true remorse. To him, the English and Anglo-Indians have become the enemy and his friendly tolerance has vanished. He now loses no opportunity to attack.

The theme of truth and deception, the sifting out of evidence about rumor and fantasy, is developed through conversations between Fielding and Hamidullah. In another attack, Hamidullah accuses Heaslop, who has brought the first news of Mrs. Moore's death, of lying about her in court. The readers now learns that she died soon after leaving Bombay and never reached Aden, as Heaslop had claimed. She had died even before the crowd began to chant her name outside the courtroom. However, there was a small bit of truth in the Indian rumor that Mrs. Moore had been sent away so that she would not testify. A short conversation between Fielding and Hamidullah emphasizes Heaslop's heedlessness in allowing her to travel in the heat, which suggests that some other motive impelled him. Fielding says that Heaslop acknowledges his imprudence, and we can assume that the son carries his share of guilt.

Mrs. Moore is the first of the characters to vanish from Chandrapore. The reasons why Mrs. Moore departed and died are a subject of controversy between the Indians and Anglo-Indians. Not every character is deeply affected by the death. Fielding and Hamidullah are relatively unmoved. Only Miss Quested, in her silence, seems "to stiffen into a monument." She will remember Mrs. Moore, and Mrs. Moore's presence will continue to exert a haunting effect on the novel.

Professor Godbole's song is another theme that continues to resonate beyond the chapter in which it is sung. In Chapter IX we learned that Aziz and Professor Godbole had both been ill after Fielding's tea party. Now, Miss Quested, too, says that she began to feel vaguely unwell after Professor Godbole's song. At first she defines the illness as sadness. Clearly, this malaise is not a physical illness. She has been touched by spiritual realities so incomprehensible to her that she is disoriented by them.

Professor Godbole sang a song of longing, a call to the god Krishna. Professor Godbole has told her that the god never comes in response to the call. For the purposes of the novel it suggests that this yearning for Divine Love and Wisdom can never be fully satisfied on earth. This form of spirituality is profoundly different from anything that Adela has ever experienced. She represents the higher ethical values of her culture, while Professor Godbole's song, distilling the essence of the spirit of India, is incompatible with the reason and order that constitute the spirit of England.

Study Questions

1. What rumor has been circulating about Miss Quested's recantation?

2. Why does Aziz feel that Fielding has deserted him?

3. What rumor does Mahmoud Ali start about Nureddin?

4. How does Dr. Panna Lal avert disaster?

5. What is the theme of the Nawab Bahadur's speech? What is ironic about his change of title?

6. What are the four possibilities Fielding suggests to account for Miss Quested's behavior? Does she seem to favor any one of them over the others?

7. What does Hamidullah mean by saying, "A great deal has been broken, more than will ever be mended"?

8. Why isn't Hamidullah impressed by Miss Quested's honesty in admitting her mistake?

9. Why does Heaslop at first remain outside on Fielding's verandah?

10. Why is Fielding horrified at Amritrao's suggestion that Miss Fielding pay 20,000 rupees in compensation?

Answers

1. The mob believes that she did not in fact recant, but was struck down by divine power for giving false testimony.

2. In aiding Miss Quested instead of remaining with his friend, Fielding seems to have gone over to the "other side."

3. He claims that he heard Major Callendar call Nureddin a "nigger" and boast of putting pepper rather than antiseptic on his wounds.

4. He publicly asks Aziz to forgive him; then he clowns, allowing the crowd to feel superior. Finally, he brings out Nureddin and shows the crowd that he is safe.

5. The Nawab Bahadur speaks of justice, courage, liberty, and prudence. He announces that he will give up his British title and be known from now on as Mr. Zulfiqar. The irony in this is that "Mr." is also a British term.

6. Fielding suggests the following: that Aziz did attempt to assault her; malice on her part; hallucination; that she was attacked by someone else. In response to Fielding's suggestion, Miss Quested assents that it might have been the guide.

7. Hamidullah means that any possibility of trust between the Indians and Anglo-Indians has been destroyed, and the social fabric of Chandrapore along with it.

8. Hamidullah has been infuriated by the overheard conversation in which Fielding and Miss Quested speculate that it could have been the guide.

9. Fielding insulted him by not standing up at the Club. Fielding understands his response as part of the social code.

10. Fielding senses that Miss Quested is going to "lose" her marriage with Heaslop; he doesn't want her to lose all her money as well.

Chapters XXVII – XXIX

New Characters:

Sir Gilbert Mellanby: *lieutenant-governor of the province*

A missionary

Summary

Fielding and Aziz lie on the roof of Mr. Zulfiqar's mansion, speculating about the future. Aziz says he will be rich from his compensation money and invites Fielding to travel with him. He brushes aside the objections he anticipates from Fielding, saying that he has become anti-British.

They discuss how much Miss Quested should pay. Fielding insists on costs only. Aziz requires an apology, suggesting half-humorously that Miss Quested admit she would have liked him to follow her into the cave. Fielding is offended on her behalf. Aziz says that he will consult Mrs. Moore. Fielding tells him she is dead.

The lieutenant-governor of the province visits and commends the outcome of the trial and Fielding's actions. He orders him to rejoin the Club. Miss Quested and Fielding write a letter of apology to Aziz. Indians want friendship rather than justice, Fielding declares.

Appealing to Mrs. Moore's memory, Fielding continues to try to talk Aziz into withdrawing his claim for excess compensation. Suddenly, he agrees to claim only costs.

Ronny Heaslop comes to tell Fielding that Miss Quested is leaving for England. Fielding goes to see her and discovers Heaslop has broken their engagement. Fielding asks her if someone had followed her into the cave or if no one had. She says it will never be known. Mrs. Moore knew, she says, and they speak of her death. They affirm their friendship and promise to write.

Adela sails home ten days later. At Port Said, she goes ashore with a missionary who tells her that every life should have a turn and a return. Suddenly, she understands that she should look up Mrs. Moore's children, Ralph and Stella, when she reaches England.

Analysis

Mrs. Moore's death and her memory shadow this entire section. At first, when Aziz declares he will consult the older woman about his demand for compensation, Fielding tries to convince Aziz that she has died. Aziz refuses to believe it. This leads the Englishman to reflect on death and how it exists within the minds of others. Later, he uses Mrs. Moore's memory in his campaign to convince Aziz to reduce his demands for compensation from Miss Quested. It is in fact Mrs. Moore's memory that finally leads Aziz to agree; he feels this is a way for him to honor her.

Fielding and Miss Quested also speak of Mrs. Moore's death and of how meditation on death may affect the living. She maintains that only Mrs. Moore would have known the solution to the central mystery: what happened in the caves. As Miss Quested disappears from India, her last resolve is to look up Mrs. Moore's children. Mrs. Moore's memory will continue to live on in Chandrapore, with the aid of a cult that has grown up around a legend.

In this section, Fielding's role as a mediator and an educator comes into play. He attempts to educate Aziz about Miss Quested's true character and to convince him to reduce his demands, while he explains to Miss Quested that she should write a letter of apology.

Again, the key to understanding between the Anglo-Indians and the Indians is true feeling. This is something Miss Quested lacked. She is sadly aware of it and actively engaged in an attempt to understand what has happened. Her growth into self-knowledge continues and deepens, extending to the realization that her engagement was not based on deep feeling. Although she was not able to break it off herself, she recognizes that his action was correct.

Divisions begin to appear in the aftermath of the crisis. Now that their solidarity in Aziz's defense is no longer necessary, the differences between Fielding and Aziz stand out. Although he feels rootless, Fielding is not ready or able to become an Indian. He is appalled by Aziz's frank awareness of his own sexual attractiveness and Miss Quested's lack of it. Although this fact has been established, speaking of it seems to outrage Fielding's British sense of modesty and decency. Aziz is no longer interested in behaving like a British gentleman, either in terms of money or of sex. His demand for compensation strikes Fielding as vindictive and excessive. Both Mrs. Moore's death and the mystery of what happened in the caves introduce reactions and metaphysical speculations that expose the limitations of rationality. The British who came to India found themselves confronted with a world that could not be confined within their concept of order and reason. In the novel, their reaction is suggested by an image that Miss Quested uses in explaining why she cannot be sure what did or did not take place in the cave. She says it is as if she were running her finger along the polished wall of the cave in the dark. This is a figurative expression of the human attempt to understand the universe through rationality alone, without the flame of the spirit.

Although Miss Quested soon withdraws the suggestion, she at first declares that Mrs. Moore would have known about the events in the cave—which she could not have witnessed visually—through telepathy. During their final conversation, Adela and Fielding, who identify themselves as rationalists, are profoundly and indefinably disturbed by a sense of something vast, a universe that dwarfs their individual concerns.

Study Questions

1. Why does Aziz say that he should have become anti-British much sooner?

2. What does Fielding try to explain about Miss Quested? On what grounds does he ask Aziz to spare her from paying excess costs?

3. Why is Fielding offended by Aziz's suggested letter of apology?

4. Why does Ronny Heaslop continue to inwardly criticize Mrs. Moore after her death?

5. Why is the letter that Fielding helps Miss Quested write a failure?

6. Why does Heaslop break off the engagement?

7. How does Miss Quested feel about her broken engagement? Why didn't she break it herself?

8. Why does Miss Quested feel that she will be alright in England?

9. Why do both Fielding and Miss Quested feel an odd sense of dissatisfaction even while they are agreeing about various topics?

10. What does the missionary's remark about a turn and a return mean to Adela Quested?

Answers

1. If Aziz had become anti-British sooner, he never would have invited the women to the Marabar Caves and thus never been imprisoned and tried.

2. Fielding points out that she is genuine and brave. She spoke out and said that she was wrong even though surrounded by Anglo-Indian friends. He appeals to Aziz to be merciful.

3. He says that it hurts him. Possibly, he is both hurt by the insult to Miss Quested and saddened to see his friend Aziz indulging in blatant self-congratulation.

4. He was unfair to her and finds it easier to compound the unfairness than to repent of it.

5. She has no real love for Aziz or the Indians, and they sense this. Fielding tells her that Indians will always prefer kindness and affection to justice.

6. He looks on her as belonging to a past he has outgrown, one connected with his earlier life in England.

7. She says it was wise of Heaslop to break the engagement; she should have broken it off herself, but that she was drifting in a state of inertia.

8. She has money, friends, and will find work. Above all, she feels that she belongs in England.

9. They have a sense of being tiny, almost insignificant. Although they do not wish to seek for larger or greater truths, some shadow of this possibility falls on them.

10. The missionary's casual remark allows her to see that her own life is at a turning point. She has turned to the East and now she is returning to the West.

Suggested Essay Topics

1. Write an essay in which you explore the effects of Mrs. Moore's death on each character and on Chandrapore as a whole.

2. Discuss the self-knowledge that Miss Quested has found in India. Has this knowledge brought her happiness? Is there a value in self-knowledge that goes beyond happiness?

Chapters XXX – XXXII

New Characters:

Major Roberts: *the new civil surgeon*

Young Milner: *the new city magistrate*

Summary

Mr. Das visits Aziz at the hospital to ask for a poem for Mr. Battacharya's new magazine. Mr. Das says he knows Aziz has a grudge against him. They finish in a half-embrace.

Aziz begins to write a poem about the decay of Islam and love. He resolves to transcend the Islamic past and attempt to love India as a whole. He will get away from British India and try for a post in a Hindu state. Hamidullah advises against it. Hamidullah winks and relays a rumor that Miss Quested was having an affair with Fielding. He wants to take Aziz behind the *purdah* curtain.

Fielding returns from a conference and Aziz picks him up from the station and tells him of the scandal: Mr. McBryde and Miss

Derek were caught having an affair. Aziz then tells him the gossip about Miss Quested. Fielding dismisses it as unimportant. Aziz scolds him about the prevalence of spies. Sensing Aziz's hostility, Fielding challenges him directly to say what is on his mind.

Aziz archly accuses him of dallying with "Madamsell Adela." Fielding is startled and so annoyed that he calls Aziz a "little rotter." Aziz is deeply hurt, but denies being offended. Fielding apologizes and tries to explain. Aziz suddenly discovers that he has a previous engagement and cannot dine with Fielding. Mr. Turton icily insists that Fielding come to the Club that night.

After Fielding's uneasy visit to the Club, during which he meets the officials who have replaced Major Callendar and Heaslop, he and Aziz have dinner together. Fielding announces that he is being sent back to England for a while.

Aziz mentions Miss Quested, asks if Fielding will see her in London, then decides it's time to leave. He refuses Fielding's offer of a ride home in his carriage and takes his bicycle instead. Aziz suspects that Fielding's real motive in going to London is to marry Miss Quested for her money. He continues to elaborate on this fantasy.

Fielding writes a letter of explanation that does not please Aziz. Aziz coldly replies that he is going to take a holiday and won't be back before Fielding leaves. He adds that he will be away at his new post when Fielding returns. After Fielding's departure, Aziz's friends encourage him in his suspicions. Soon Aziz has convinced himself that Fielding has married Miss Quested.

During the trip back to England, Fielding rediscovers a harmonious beauty in Egypt, Crete, and Venice. In Venice, particularly, he appreciates the joys of form. He thinks of the Mediterranean as the human norm and the southern exit from it as leading to the monstrous and extraordinary.

Analysis

In this closing section of Part II, the theme of division and departure is elaborated. As Aziz's suspicion of Fielding grows, he and Fielding come close to an open break. Aziz archly calls Fielding a "naughty boy." Annoyed, Fielding calls him a "little rotter." The social distance between them gives an entirely different weight to the two terms. While Aziz has been playful, Fielding's use of schoolboy slang reveals that he thinks of Aziz more as a boy than a man. Aziz is plainly and painfully aware of the disrespect implied in this expression. The differences between the two men are evident; the fact that Aziz has believed the rumor about Miss Quested demonstrates that he does not know what Fielding's standards of behavior are. Since Aziz associates British rule with treachery, he cannot believe that this particular Englishman might be unwilling to betray a friend.

At dinner later, they speak of poetry and religion. Aziz says that poetry has lost the power of making men brave. Fielding agrees that poetry should touch life, but says that patriotic poetry is not possible in a fragmented India. They then pass on to a sister subject: religion. Aziz refers to his earlier self, the one who took everyone as a friend. He relates this to the Persian expression: the Friend, a way of referring to God. Aziz, who has previously been so moved by thoughts of Islam, now says he does not want to be a religious poet. And Fielding, who is a declared atheist, insists that there is something in religion that may be true. It has not yet been expressed, he says, but perhaps the Hindus have discovered it. This is the first sign that Fielding has any leanings toward spirituality. His dawning sense of wonder about Hindu religion will be further developed in Part III.

Fielding's actual departure brings a shift of perspective. Within India, the novel has alternated between the perspective of the Indians and the Anglo-Indians, and set both of these against the larger perspective of Nature and the Universe. Now, as Fielding lands in different ports during his journey home, he comes to see India as strange, misshapen, almost monstrous. His sense of beauty was originally shaped by Mediterranean and European standards and he is glad, though half-guilty, to discover them again.

In his absence, Fielding's Indian friends have begun to feel that he is a traitor. Aziz has convinced himself that Fielding tricked him about the money and that he has married Miss Quested. It is on this note of division that Part II comes to a close. The three English people who seemed to be exceptions to the prevailing attitude of superiority have left India. Fielding's experience in returning to the Club has shown that those Anglo-Indians who are left, even the newcomers, have not changed. The Indians themselves, even Hamidullah, have closed ranks against them.

Study Questions

1. How do Aziz and Mr. Das feel about each other during their outwardly friendly conversation?

2. Why does Aziz resolve to leave British India and to go live in a Hindu state?

3. What is the "naughty rumor" Mohammed Latif is spreading?

4. Does Hamidullah insist that his wife keep *purdah*, or is it her choice?

5. What is Fielding's reaction when Aziz tells him about the rumor that Mohammed Latif is spreading?

6. Why does Aziz claim to have remembered a previous dinner engagement with Mr. Das?

7. According to Fielding, why is it difficult for Indians to write poetry?

8. Why is Aziz, who is not a mercenary man, haunted by the thought of the 20,000 rupees he did not claim from Miss Quested?

9. What is Aziz's most extreme fantasy about Fielding and Miss Quested, the one he comes to accept as fact?

10. Why does Fielding feel a sense of disloyalty while he is appreciating the beauty of Venice?

Answers

1. Aziz wishes that Hindus did not remind him of cow-dung, while Mr. Das thinks to himself that some Muslims are very violent.

2. He wants to escape from British India and believes once outside it, he will be able to write poetry again.

3. Mohammed Latif claims to have heard that Fielding is having an affair with Miss Quested.

4. Although the Muslim women claimed that they would give up *purdah* during Aziz's trial, the Begum Hamidullah invents excuses for not seeing Fielding. Hamidullah believes that Indian women actually make their own decisions.

5. Fielding says it is unimportant and begins to explain why it is not true.

6. Aziz has been deeply insulted by Fielding's calling him a "little rotter." He invents another engagement to avoid having to dine with Fielding.

7. Fielding tells Aziz that Indians cannot go on repeating the tired clichés of traditional poetry, and, since India is not unified under one government, truly patriotic or nationalistic poetry is impossible.

8. Aziz cannot forget the money because he feels that he was tricked about it.

9. Aziz convinces himself that Fielding talked him out of claiming a large compensation so that he could marry Miss Quested for her money. Aziz believes that they have gotten married.

10. Fielding has been in India for some time, and feels that he is criticizing his home by praising the beauty of Venice.

Suggested Essay Topics

1. How does the misunderstanding between Aziz and Fielding exemplify the distance between the cultures they each belong to? How and why has each offended the other? Explain.

2. Aziz tells Fielding that he was a child when they first met. Explain what he means by this. Write an essay analyzing the ways in which Aziz has changed.

Part III: The Temple
Chapter XXXIII

New Character:

The Rajah of Mau: *an old Hindu ruler*

Summary

When Part III opens, two years have passed since Fielding left India. The setting is now the Hindu state of Mau, where Professor Godbole and Dr. Aziz live. Professor Godbole and his choir are performing at the Hindu festival celebrating Shri Krishna's birthday. The courtyard at Mau is filled with Hindu worshippers. There is music from many sources. In this setting, a small Europeanized band is almost unnoticeable.

Professor Godbole calls his musicians to a new rhythm. While he and his musicians melt into universal love, the professor remembers an old woman he had met in Chandrapore. When this memory comes to him, he transports her to a place of completion through his spiritual force. In that place, there is room even for a wasp. Professor Godbole is dancing on a strip of red carpet, lost in ecstasy.

At this juncture, a *litter* bearing the Rajah appears. His attendants seat him against a pillar. The Brahmin brings out a model of the village where Krishna was born, along with the figures who play a part in the birth legend. When the clock strikes midnight, the conch is blown, elephants trumpet, packets of colored powder are thrown at the altar, and shouts are heard. Sorrow vanishes; nothing remains but an all-embracing joy. The experience is beyond thought or memory.

Next, a paper-maché cobra and a wooden cradle appear. Professor Godbole holds the red silk napkin that represents the god. Godbole hands it to the Rajah, who baptizes it, tears pouring from his eyes. He is carried away and put in the care of his other physician, Dr. Aziz.

Down in the courtyard, there is laughter and games are played. The narrator tells us that this worship, unlike Christianity, succeeds in including merriment. One by one, children are chosen from the crowd to be caressed and treated as Shri Krishna. The games continue.

The narrator reminds us that the literal truth of this reenact-ment cannot be established. It does not matter; all birth may be an allegory. To Professor Godbole, the fact that Mrs. Moore was a Christian and he is a Brahmin Hindu does not matter either. He, in effect, becomes God and loves her as God would love her. In a double transformation, he also becomes Mrs. Moore, and beseeches God to come.

Analysis

The presence of the spiritual, which has made itself felt in varying ways throughout the novel, is now at centerstage. The traditional re-enactment of Krishna's birth is performed in the courtyard at Mau. The action takes place outside of time and space, in the presence of God. Unlike Christians, Hindus believe that there have been and will continue to be many incarnations; the joyous celebration of Krishna's birth might be compared to Christmas. The narrator draws some explicit parallels between the legend of Krishna's birth and of Christ's.

In India everything seems different. The central message common to both traditions, "God is Love," appears as "God si Love," hinting at a reversal that might stand for an India as seen through Western eyes. On one level it indicates that to understand India, Westerners must begin with its tradition of ecstatic devotional religion. On a simpler and more basic level, they must begin by loving the country and the Indians themselves. They will have to confront unfamiliarity, yet it may be that India offers them a mirror image of themselves.

The colorful and crowded spectacle of Hindu India, which contrasts with the Anglo-Indian enclave in Chandrapore, is displayed in the scene at Mau. Just as the jumble of objects on the altar almost conceals the image of the god himself, the accumu-lation of people, sounds, and sights in the courtyard overwhelms the spectator. On the red carpet, in the midst of this seeming chaos, Professor Godbole dances in a trance of religious ecstasy. His outer senses dim; he abandons logic and deliberate effort and surrenders himself to universal love.

This character, who has been somewhat aloof and elusive in the previous chapters of the novel, has now left the alien setting of the civil station and is on his home ground. The action he performs in "imitating God" and elevating Mrs. Moore to a state of spiritual completion is difficult to describe and to comprehend. Its nearest counterpart in Christianity might be in prayers that are said for the release of the spirit. The subtle aftereffects of this transcendence, however, can be perceived throughout the final section of the novel.

In this fully Hindu setting, transcendence has been achieved and brought to completion. Although, transforming himself into Mrs. Moore, Godbole beseeches God to come, there is a crucial difference between this scene and the song of longing he sang at Fielding's party. That earlier song affected those who heard it with a kind of lingering malaise. In contrast, this scene is filled with joy. The division and conflict that have marked the plot so far have disappeared.

All individuality disappears from the faces of the worshippers as well; all reason, form, and beauty disappear from the scene. The principal values of Western civilization are annihilated. Yet something arguably greater takes their place: transcendent joy and a sense of union in which all differences and divisions vanish. Again, the point of view of the earlier chapters has now expanded to include all those shadowy, hovering suggestions of realities beyond his grasp. The voice of the narrator is now the reader's guide.

Study Questions

1. How much time has passed since Fielding left India?

2. What is Professor Godbole's title in Mau?

3. What is the expression on the faces of the worshippers when they see the image of Shri Krishna?

4. Why are Godbole's musicians unperturbed by the Europeanized band?

5. Does Professor Godbole make an effort to remember Mrs. Moore for a particular reason?

6. Who is the ruler of the State of Mau? What is his role in the festival?

7. According to legend, at what time was Shri Krishna born?

8. Who are the two physicians who take care of the Rajah?

9. What games are played after the Rajah has been carried away?

10. What are Professor Godbole's thoughts after the festival?

Answers

1. Two years.

2. He is the minister of education.

3. Their faces wear a beautiful and radiant expression, an impersonal beauty that makes them all resemble each other.

4. They are in a state beyond competition.

5. No. She simply floats into his head, along with other memories.

6. The Hindu Rajah. He must say, "I name this child Shri Krishna," and put it into the cradle.

7. Krishna was born at midnight.

8. A Hindu physician and Dr. Aziz.

9. Children are carried around and treated like gods. Later, a large jar is hung and hit with sticks until it breaks and rains a sort of rice pudding over the children.

10. He realizes that he has seen Mrs. Moore and the wasp, and around her clinging forms of trouble. In placing himself in the position of God and including her in love, he has done all that he could do.

Suggested Essay Topics

1. Forster describes the ceremony as the annihilation of reason, form, and beauty. Yet it is also presented as a celebration of God's love. Are these concepts compatible? Explain Forster's position and then present your own evaluation.

2. Professor Godbole is depicted in a state of religious ecstasy. According to this chapter, what are the characteristics of this state? In what sense is Professor Godbole imitating God?

Chapters XXXIV – XXXV

New Characters:

Colonel Maggs: *Anglo-Indian political agent, an opponent of Aziz*

Jemila, Ahmed, and Karim: *Aziz's children*

Ralph Moore: *Fielding's brother-in-law, Mrs. Moore's son*

Summary

Dr. Aziz leaves the palace the next morning to return to his house. He sees Godbole, but the devotee indicates he does not want to be disturbed. Absent-mindedly, Godbole tells Aziz that "he" has arrived at the European Guest House. Knowing that Fielding is coming on an official visit, and that he has married, Aziz understands that this refers to Fielding. Holding to his old mistake, Aziz assumes his wife is Miss Quested.

We learn that while he was still in Chandrapore, he had received a letter from Fielding telling of his approaching marriage. Aziz had tossed the letter to Mahmoud Ali, telling him to answer it, and had destroyed subsequent letters.

Aziz lives in Mau, with a woman, and has his children with him. He is tolerated in this Hindu state, but does have one enemy in Colonel Maggs, the British Political Agent from the Criminal Investigation Department. However, the Viceroy's policy has changed, and British influence now has less weight; the Rajah refuses to dismiss Aziz.

Aziz tears up the note in which Fielding tells him he is coming with his wife and her brother and requests help in supplying things for the State Guest House and in complying with court etiquette. He wants to avoid seeing the visitors.

The morning after the Krishna celebration, Aziz takes his children with him to visit the shrine of an Islamic saint. Inside the Shrine of the Head are many bees' nests, but the children are not stung. Aziz and the children go on to visit a tiny mosque and then wander over an old deserted fort, where they meet with a line of prisoners. Referring to a ritual that will be reenacted during the Krishna procession that night, the boys ask them which one will be pardoned. One prisoner inquires about the Rajah's health. Aziz tells him that it is always improving, although in fact, the Rajah died after the ceremony. In order not to dim the festival, the death is being concealed

The children see Fielding and his brother-in-law below. When the two Englishmen enter the shrine, they are attacked by bees and rush out again. Aziz's mood improves. He shouts to them, advising the brother-in-law, who has been stung, to stay away from him and lie down in a pool of water. It has begun to rain. Aziz pulls some stings from the man's wrists, and speaks roughly to him.

Fielding calls to Aziz in unfriendly tones and asks why his letters have not been answered. It rains harder and Fielding imperatively suggests that Aziz accompany them to their carriage. Fielding begins to complain sternly of the lack of hospitality at the Guest House. He tells Aziz that they want to see the torchlight procession that night.

When they reach the carriage, Aziz says, "Jump in, Mr. Quested...." Fielding replies, "Who on earth is Mr. Quested?" Aziz's mistake is revealed, and he pales. Fielding is friendly, scathing, and scornful all at once. Aziz's shame turns to rage and he declares that he wants nothing to do with the English.

Analysis

This concluding section of the novel takes place in the season after the welcome monsoon rains have come. The rains bring not only relief from the heat, but also fertility to the fields and prosperity to human beings.

This chapter, which begins on the morning after the festival, explores the world of secular power. This is a Hindu state. Furthermore, it seems that British policy has changed and these states are now allowed more control over their own affairs. This annoys Colonel Maggs, the British political agent who would like to harass Aziz. Aziz feels secure in Mau. He is living with a woman and has his children with him. He is in charge of the hospital and has been the Rajah's personal physician. Now the Rajah is dead, and no one yet knows what his successor will be like. This hints at possible change, but Aziz is not greatly concerned.

Although he is not a Hindu, the site of Aziz's first meeting with Fielding suggests that the doctor is now on his own ground. Aziz, who has tried to avoid meeting Fielding, is at an old fort containing the Muslim Shrine of the Head and a small mosque. Thus, it is a parallel to Aziz's first meeting with Mrs. Moore at the mosque. There, the two strangers had opened their hearts to one another. Here at the fort, with its military connotations, the two friends meet as adversaries. As if to signal this, a swarm of bees attack the Englishmen.

The change in Aziz has already been indicated by his tearing up the note Fielding sends him after arriving at the Guest House. Aziz has a new sense of power and has flouted hospitality, which was once his cardinal virtue. He ignores even basic requests from Fielding. In climbing the hill to the fort, Fielding's party symbolically suggests the invasion of India by the British.

The attack by a swarm of bees immediately puts the English at a disadvantage. Aziz is pleased. He demonstrates his new sense of power, and his old resentment, by his offhand approach to Fielding and his condescending treatment of Ralph Moore. Fielding complains of the contrast between the hospitable reception they have received in other Hindu states and the inattentiveness shown in Mau.

Another element of the plot is resolved when this meeting finally reveals that Mahmoud Ali has duped Aziz, and that Aziz's dark suspicions of Fielding are unwarranted. When Aziz discovers that Fielding's wife is actually Mrs. Moore's daughter, and not Miss Quested, he is mortified by his mistake. Instead of apologizing, he allows his shame to turn to anger and shouts that he wants nothing more to do with the English. This open fury, too, indicates that Aziz is now able to behave toward Fielding like an equal, not like a subject under British rule.

When he calms down, he realizes that hearing the name of Mrs. Moore/Esmiss Esmoor has had a curious effect on him. He feels as if she had come to help him. Transfigured by her death, Mrs. Moore's spirit is able to transcend the barriers of ethnic conflict that separate the living from each other.

Study Questions

1. Is Aziz tolerated in this Hindu state? What is the most important distinction there?

2. Why doesn't Aziz know that Fielding has married Mrs. Moore's daughter?

3. How has Aziz's life changed since he left Chandrapore?

4. Who is Colonel Maggs? Why is he unable to influence the Rajah against Aziz?

5. Why does Aziz tear up Fielding's note?

6. Why is the news of the Rajah's death concealed?

7. Who is and who is not stung inside the Shrine of the Head?

8. What conditions at the Guest House cause Fielding to complain?

9. What reveals Aziz's mistake about Fielding's marriage?

10. What is Aziz's reaction?

Answers

1. Aziz is tolerated in this Hindu state, where the greatest division is between Brahmin and non-Brahmin, the highest caste Hindus and the lower castes.

2. When the letter arrived in Chandrapore, Aziz read only the first lines, then tossed it to Mahmoud Ali to answer. Aziz tore up all of Fielding's other letters.

3. Aziz now lives with a woman and has his children with him. He runs the small hospital himself, instead of working under an Anglo-Indian.

4. Colonel Maggs is the political agent. It seems that the British Viceroy has changed policy and the Hindu rulers are aware that the political agent no longer has much power over them.

5. Aziz assumes that Miss Quested is the woman Fielding married; he wants nothing to do with the couple.

6. The news of the Rajah's death is concealed so that the festival can proceed joyfully.

7. Fielding's brother-in-law is stung; Aziz's son Ahmed, who entered earlier, was not stung.

8. There are no eggs and the mosquito nets are torn. They want to go out in a boat, but cannot find the oars.

9. Aziz addresses Fielding's brother-in-law as "Mr. Quested."

10. Filled with shame and rage, he turns pale.

Suggested Essay Topics

1. Hospitality has been a major theme in the minds of the Indian characters in this book. Describe the hospitality—or lack of it—that Fielding is offered in Mau. What accounts for his treatment?

2. Describe the character of Aziz as he appears in this section. How would you assess the changes that have occurred in him?

Chapter XXXVI

New Characters:

A young woman singer

Stella Moore: *Fielding's wife, Mrs. Moore's daughter*

Summary

The palace continues to hum. Although the customary dramatic performance depicting the legend of Krishna will not take place, the festival has still created an atmosphere of love and peace. Since Mau is usually a site of suspicion and selfishness, Aziz finds the change difficult to comprehend.

Around evening, he remembers the ointment he had promised to send to the Guest House and decides to ride over to deliver it. On the way, he sees the procession forming and almost bumps into Professor Godbole. It turns out that Godbole has known for over a year that Fielding married Heaslop's sister. Godbole smiles and asks Aziz not to be angry with him for not informing him. The *Sweeper's* band is arriving and when the doors are thrown open, the whole

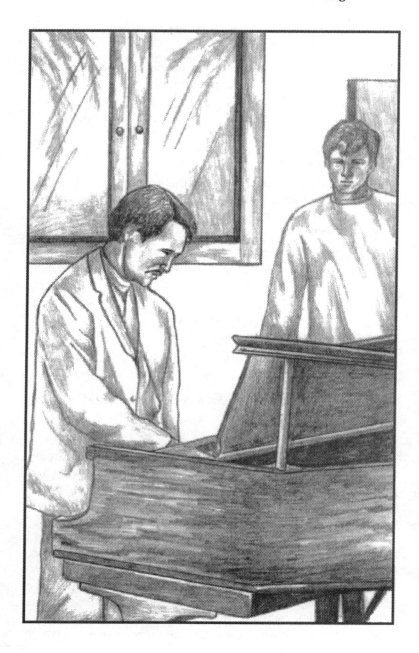

court can be seen inside; the Ark of the Lord stands in the fairway. Slightly bored, Aziz rides on out of town and stops by the Mau *tank*. In the center of it, looking like a small black blot, he can see the Guest House boat. Continuing on his way, he reaches the European Guest House, 200 feet above the water.

Aziz goes through the rooms and reads two letters lying on the piano. One is from Heaslop to Fielding, apologizing for having been unreasonable and referring to a "son and heir." The second is from Miss Quested to Mrs. Fielding; friendly and sensible, it mentions "my debt which I will never repay in person."

The State guns are fired and a rocket set off, signaling the release of the prisoner. The choir's song penetrates the House. Aziz and Ralph move out onto the porch, where Aziz holds out his hand and speaks gently. Ralph replies that he can always tell whether a stranger is his friend.

Both acknowledge that the two nations cannot be friends. Ralph tells him that Mrs. Moore had spoken of him in her letters, and that she loved him. Aziz feels gratitude, but cannot account for it. He proposes to take Ralph out on the water and finds the place where the oars are hidden. There is a sudden flash of lightning. Ralph tells Aziz to row back and they see the image of a king under a canopy. Aziz tells Ralph that the Rajah is dead. What they have seen is an image of the Rajah's dead father.

Ralph asks Aziz to row nearer, and Aziz obeys. The chant of Radhakrishna changes, and Aziz believes he hears the "syllables of salvation" that had been chanted during his trial at Chandrapore. He rows nearer, until the palanquin of Krishna appears, surrounded by singers. Godbole sees the boat and waves at them. An image of Krishna's birthplace is about to be thrown into the water.

Suddenly, English voices cry out; the two boats collide. The servitor's tray, part of the final act of the festival, strikes the English. The boats capsize; everything, including the servitor's tray and the two letters, float away.

Analysis

In this chapter, the narrator informs us that "Religion is a living force in Hindu life." The entire chapter is an illustration of this statement. The all-pervading atmosphere of the festival affects even those, like Aziz, who do not believe in Krishna. Instead of indulging in intrigue, the rival claimants to the throne are careful not to disturb the atmosphere of peace and love. Preparations for the torchlight procession are beginning. Gods are mounting the floats.

Religious divisions are indicated and then bridged during the festival. In the midst of it, Aziz almost bumps into Godbole, which would have contaminated the Brahmin. Godbole apologizes for not telling Aziz about Fielding's wife, which he has known for some time. He declares that he is, within his limitations, Aziz's true friend, and reminds Aziz that this is his holy festival. Aziz smiles at him, another indication of the way in which the festival calms all resentments.

A prime characteristic of Hinduism is that it favors inclusion over exclusion. The caste system was strict and exclusive at that time, yet the *Sweeper's* band is integral to the festival. When it appears, only its music will open the doors to the revelation of the Ark of the Lord.

For a while, Aziz is still gripped by his rancorous memories. Reading the letters from Heaslop and Miss Quested in the Guest House reminds him further of Chandrapore. Aziz is still occupied with trying to right his wrongs, which entails a reversal.

Inflamed by memories, he persecutes Ralph for a while. There are two reasons why his attitude and his manner change. One is Ralph's own character; he is not the type of a bullying Englishman. Instead, he is strange, frail, and sensitive. He speaks to Aziz from emotional truth, not verbal truth, cutting through the other's sneering attack by simply claiming, "Dr. Aziz, we have done you no harm." Aziz is, of course, persecuting Ralph in his identity as a member of a group-the British in India-and ignoring him as an individual. He has just begun to perceive him as an individual when a chant from the festival permeates the Guest House.

It is a chant of reversal and of union: Krishnaradha, Radhakrishna, and it enters the house like "rumours of salvation." Its effect is to remind Aziz of something beyond the caves. He repents of his earlier nastiness and speaks gently to Ralph. Aziz finds himself remembering Mrs. Moore, the mosque, and the beginning of the cycle. This time, Ralph reminds him that Mrs. Moore loved him. He now honors Ralph as Mrs. Moore's son.

Once again, it is through the effects of spiritual rhythm and music that a character's mood is altered and human differences resolved. The power of the mantra is well known in India and is practiced in order to produce spiritual transformation.

In the last scene, all the antagonisms and misunderstandings that have divided the cultures and the characters dissolve, and everything mingles together. The four outsiders collide with each other, and with the servitor's tray. It is Stella who capsizes the two boats, rocking back and forth between Fielding and Aziz as she symbolically brings them together. Like her mother, she has collapsed the division between the Indians and the Anglo-Indians. Memories of the past float away along with the letters. As the villagers straggle back to their homes, they are still singing. Again the narrator repeats: "God si love."

Study Questions

1. Why doesn't the usual dramatic performance depicting the life of Krishna take place?

2. Why is it difficult for Aziz to understand the atmosphere that surrounds the festival?

3. Why does Aziz intend to bring the ointment back with him after treating Ralph? Why does he change his mind?

4. What is the *Sweeper's* band? What is its function in the festival?

5. Who are the letters from and what do they say?

6. Why is Aziz rough with Ralph at first? When and why does his attitude change?

7. Why is Aziz puzzled by his gratitude toward Mrs. Moore?

8. What is the place that Ralph directs Aziz toward in the boat?

9. What are the "syllables of salvation" Aziz hears when the chant changes?

10. What upsets the two boats?

Answers

1. It is traditionally performed in front of the Rajah, who is dead.

2. As a Muslim, Aziz does not participate. He is also aware of the suspicion and selfishness that characterize Mau for most of the year, and does not understand how these could have been suspended.

3. Aziz changes his mind when he begins to see Ralph as Mrs. Moore's son. He wants to give him a present in acknowledgment, and the ointment is the only one available.

4. The *Sweepers* are Untouchables, the lowest caste in India. This is a moment reserved for the despised and rejected. All other music is silenced; it is their tune alone that will bring the god out of his house.

5. The letters are from Heaslop and Miss Quested. Heaslop's indicates that he wants to make up a quarrel with Fielding. Miss Quested's shows concern for Ralph Moore and a sense of a debt that she owes to India.

6. Aziz is still angry and ashamed. He perceives Ralph as weak, and this increases his cruelty. Then the chanting reaches his ears. The mood changes, and Ralph's perceptiveness reminds Aziz of Mrs. Moore.

7. Aziz knows that Mrs. Moore did not actually do anything tangible for him.

8. He directs him toward an effigy of the Rajah's dead father.

9. For Aziz, the syllables of salvation are "Esmiss Esmoor," the chant that preceded Miss Quested's recantation at the trial.

10. The two boats capsize when Stella moves back and forth between Fielding and Aziz.

Suggested Essay Topics

1. Trace the role that music and chanting play in this chapter and what functions they perform, both within the ritual and beyond it.

2. Write a character portrait of Ralph Moore.

Chapter XXXVII

Summary

Fielding and Aziz go for their last ride together in the Mau jungles. The Rajah's death has been announced. From the official point of view, the visit is a failure. Every day Godbole has promised to show Fielding the high school, but has always made some excuse. Now Aziz tells him that the school has been converted into a granary. The school only exists on paper.

Fielding feels that the visit has been a success in terms of friendship. He and Aziz have resumed their old relationship. They look around at the bright scenery and see a cobra. When they stop to let it pass, Aziz shows Fielding a charming letter he wants to send Miss Quested, expressing his gratitude. Fielding is pleased. Aziz apologizes for his old suspicions. Fielding suggests that Aziz talk to Stella, who also believes the incident at the caves and all its repercussions have been expunged.

They both know that this is good-bye, since there seems to be no place left for their friendship. Fielding has now become a part of Anglo-India. He is not sure he would be able to defy his own people again as he did before.

Fielding speaks again of the calm that Mau has brought his wife. He asks Aziz about the Krishna festival. Aziz knows little of it besides its name. Fielding explains that he wants to discover its spiritual side. Aziz still professes ignorance and indifference to Hindu reactions. Fielding tells Aziz that he wants to understand why Ralph and Stella are drawn to Hinduism, though not to its outward forms.

Aziz resists Fielding's attempts to connect him to Ralph and Stella. He adds a line to the letter to Miss Quested, telling her that from now on he will remember her along with the sacred name of Mrs. Moore.

They argue about politics all the way back to Mau. Fielding maintains that without the British, things fall apart in India. He accuses Aziz of forgetting his medicine and going back to charms. He also scoffs at the theme of Aziz's poems. For his part, Aziz wants to see the British thrown out of India. He tells Fielding that when England is in difficulties, in the next European war, it will be time

for the Indians. Aziz promises that if his own generation cannot expel the English, his children's generation will. The two men embrace, acknowledging that they both want friendship.

Analysis

Although the facts may never be known, the incident in the caves has mysteriously been resolved. Both Aziz and Stella, in different ways, are aware that the past has been put to rest. The meeting between Fielding and Aziz, and between Aziz and Ralph, has obviously contributed to clearing up misunderstandings. Remembering what took place during Godbole's dance, we must add that his ecstatic transformation of Mrs. Moore also dispelled the shadows he had perceived as clinging around her spirit. Those clinging shadows had affected everyone and everything connected with the original trial.

This final chapter continues to explore the theme of Hindu mysticism. It is surprising to find that Fielding, the self-described rationalist and atheist, is now the one who insists on questioning Aziz about the Krishna festival. Aziz, who identified with Islam and religious poetry, has previously declared he did not want to be a religious poet. Now he is bored by the topic of spirituality. This is a Hindu festival, yet the idea of an unattainable God who is both with and without attributes is basic to Islam. For Forster's purposes, it was necessary to alter Aziz's character along pragmatic and political lines.

At first, Fielding believes that since Aziz is an Oriental, he will have a spiritual understanding, and attempts to bring him together with Ralph and Stella. Aziz makes his lack of interest clear. Fielding acknowledges that both his wife and her brother have an inner tranquility and an access to spiritual realities that he lacks. He draws a distinction between these two, who are spiritual seekers, and himself, Miss Quested, and Aziz, who are not.

Sustained by their renewed friendship, Fielding and Aziz are able to confront each other directly. Fielding has become a conservative. Although he earlier refused to endorse the formula: "England holds India for her good," he now believes in the necessity of British rule for India. He has begun to identify with the Anglo-Indians and finds it hard to believe that he once defied them. The reversal that has taken place in Aziz has also taken place in Fielding; their opposing loyalties are now sharply defined.

Now that Fielding and Aziz are on opposite sides, they express their opposing views on British rule in India. Fielding jeers that India slips into superstition and backwardness when not directly under British supervision. Aziz's statement that the Indians' time will come when the British go to war is an implied threat, hinting that the Indians will not stand by them.

Politics give way to a reaffirmation of friendship as the two men embrace and affirm their affection for each other. Geography and politics, however, ensure that this friendship has no place in the world as it is when the novel ends.

Study Questions

1. Why do Fielding and the others have to leave Mau so soon?

2. Why hasn't Professor Godbole shown Fielding around the high school?

3. In what sense has Fielding's visit been a failure? In what sense has it been a success?

4. What does Aziz say in his letter to Miss Quested?

5. Why does Fielding want Aziz to talk to Stella or to Ralph?

6. What question does Fielding ask himself when he reflects on the events surrounding the trial?

7. Why does Fielding persist in questioning Aziz about the Krishna festival?

8. What is Aziz's visionary experience?

9. During their playful quarrel, Fielding makes fun of Aziz. What does he choose to ridicule about Aziz?

10. What is Fielding's position now on British rule in India? What is Aziz's position?

Answers

1. The State is officially in mourning, now that the Rajah's death has been announced.

2. The school has been converted into a granary, and Godbole is embarrassed to admit it.

3. In terms of his official mission, the visit is a failure because he has not been able to inspect the school. In personal terms, it is a success because of the resumption of a friendship with Aziz.

4. Aziz tells her that thanks to her, he is able to live happily in Mau with his children instead of in jail.

5. Fielding knows that Ralph and Stella have a mystical sense that he lacks. Identifying Aziz as a mystical Indian, he feels Aziz may be able to understand it and explain it to him.

6. He asks himself whether he would have the courage to defy the Anglo-Indians again, since he now feels that he is one of them.

7. Fielding believes that if he can understand the Krishna festival, he will have some clue to Stella and Ralph's attitude toward Hindu spirituality.

8. Aziz suddenly sees butterflies everywhere; he then hears in his mind a poem about Mecca and about the thornbushes that await pilgrims who have not seen God the Friend before they die.

9. Fielding criticizes Aziz for going back to charms instead of Western medicine, saying that this is an example of how India goes to seed without British supervision.

10. Fielding now believes that British rule is necessary for India. Aziz is determined that either his own or his children's generation will expel the British.

Suggested Essay Topics

1. Taking Ralph and Stella as projections of Mrs. Moore, how do they reflect some of her qualities? In what ways have they gone beyond their mother? Do they affect others in the way their mother did? Give examples.

2. Discuss Aziz's dreams of emancipation from British rule in light of what actually happened before and after India became independent. Considering that Indian troops fought both for and against the Allies in World War II, and that India gained its independence shortly after it, was his remark about the next European war prophetic?

Sample Analytical Paper Topics

Topic #1

In a 1938 essay, Forster declared, "…if I had to choose between betraying my country and betraying my friend, I hope I should have the guts to betray my country." Demonstrate the ways in which Fielding's actions in the novel are consistent with this statement.

Outline

I.   Thesis Statement: A Passage to India *illustrates the paramount value of friendship, even when it conflicts with group loyalty.*

II. Fielding's friendship with Aziz must surmount many obstacles

    A.   The cultural and ethnic gap between them, reinforced by social structures

    B.   Many acquaintances attempt to undermine the friendship

    C.   They frequently misunderstand each other

III. Although other Anglo-Indians brand Fielding as a traitor, he sides with Aziz

    A.   He believes Aziz is innocent

    B.   He defies his own group to defend Aziz

IV.   The friendship between Aziz and Fielding survives rumors and years of separation

  A.   After they are reunited, Aziz abandons his suspicious attitude

  B.   Fielding forgives him

  C.   Their friendship is so strong that it allows for conflict based on their differing group identities

  D.   Although the time and place will not allow their friendship to flourish, both men acknowledge the strength of their bond

Topic #2

Miss Quested repeatedly says that the mystery of what happened in the caves will never be solved. Some readers believed that Aziz might have been guilty of an assault, or at least a sexual advance, on her. Use the facts presented in the novel, and its narrative technique, to refute this charge.

Outline

I.   Thesis Statement: *A close reading of* A Passage to India *demonstrates that, whether or not Miss Quested was assaulted in the caves, Aziz was not the perpetrator.*

II.   Mrs. Moore says that it is not in Aziz's character to do such a thing

  A.   Aziz's idea of hospitality would prevent him from insulting a guest

  B.   Aziz is too practical and unsentimental about sex to take a risk

  C.   Miss Quested states that only Mrs. Moore knows the answer

III. It is unlikely because Aziz has other sexual outlets, and finds Miss Quested unattractive

  A.   He is planning a trip to Calcutta for sexual purposes

  B.   In a conversation with Fielding, Aziz refers to Miss Quested's lack of sexual charms

IV. Aziz's version of the events is more complete and convincing than other versions

    A. The narrative follows Aziz at the caves

    B. Miss Quested's experience remains inconclusive

    C. Fielding's attempted reconstruction of the events raises the possibility of an attack by Aziz but does not explore it

Topic #3

In *An Autobiography*, the president of India, Jawahlarl Nehru, wrote of the Anglo-Indians, "They lived in a narrow, circumscribed world of their own—Anglo-India—which was neither England nor India." For his part, Forster once wrote that every Englishman in India felt and behaved as if he were a member of an army of occupation. Use examples from *A Passage to India* to illustrate these observations.

Outline

I. Thesis Statement: *Despite their attempts to re-create England in India, the Anglo-Indians behaved like an army of occupation on foreign territory.*

II. The Anglo-Indians attempted to recreate England in India

    A. The houses were adaptations of English-style bungalows

    B. Their social life centered around the English club

III. The Anglo-Indians could not recreate England because they could not do without the Indians

    A. The Anglo-Indians were obsessed with the need to keep the Indians under control

    B. They maintained superior rank and allowed the Indians to work only as subordinates

IV. Mr. Turton and Major Callendar are examples of a colonial mentality

    A. Mr. Turton calls for justice, but regards all Indians as inferiors

B. Major Callendar is openly racist and believes in calling out the army rather than relying on the rule of law

V. Even Fielding, who has taken a different attitude from the other Anglo-Indians, betrays a sense of superiority

A. In a moment of annoyance, he calls Aziz a "little rotter"

B. By the end of the novel, he is convinced that India needs British rule to maintain order and progress

SECTION FOUR

Appendix

Glossary of Anglo-Indian Terminology

Anglo-Indian: An English person living in India, particularly one there for a considerable time.

Aryan Brother: Aryan originally referred to the eastern part of ancient Persia; also to the family of Indo-European languages and anyone descended from the ancient people who spoke one of them. The term "Aryan Brother" was an ironic and disparaging term Anglo-Indians applied to Indians.

babu, babuism: Originally a Hindu title of respect; among Anglo-Indians, used to refer to a native clerk or official who could write English; sometimes applied disparagingly to a Hindu with a superficial English education.

badmash: Delinquent, rogue.

bazaar: Originally, a market place consisting of ranges of shops or stalls where merchandise is offered for sale.

begum: A queen, princess, or lady of high rank in India.

bhang: Native name for a highly intoxicating Indian variety of common hemp, sometimes extended to refer to hashish.

Brahmin: Member of the highest or priestly cast.

Brahminy bull: A bull dedicated to Shiva and then set loose; a humped Indian ox.

caaba (more often **Kaaba**): Sacred edifice at Mecca containing the venerated "black stone," the most sacred place in Islam.

chhatri (more often **chatra**): Silk umbrella like a little tent roof on a cane handle.

chit: Letter or note; order for a drink.

chunam: Cement or plaster made of shell-lime or sea-sand, used in India.

chuprassie (also **chaprassy**): Messenger, orderly, servant.

dak bungalow: resthouse for travelers, maintained by the government, with primitive accomodations.

dhoti: Loin cloth worn by Hindus; a long narrow cloth wound around the body, passed between the thighs, and tucked in under the waistband behind.

Eurasian: Of mixed European and Asiatic (usually Indian) parentage.

fez: A skullcap of felt, of a dull crimson color in the form of a truncated cone, ornamented with a long black tassel; the national headdress of the Turks.

hakim: A judge, ruler, or governor in Mohammedan countries; in India, the administrative authority in a district. Also, Muslim doctor.

hammam: "Turkish bath." Oriental bathing establishment.

Huzoor (from Arabic **huzor,** presence): title of respect; Your Honor.

izzat: Honor, prestige, self-esteem.

maidan: An open space in or near a town, parade-ground.

maharajah: Title of certain Indian princes.

maharani: Wife of a maharajah, sometimes shortened to rani.

mahatma: Great soul.

memsahib: European married woman. A compound word based on Ma'am and Sahib.

Mohurram: Islamic festival of fasting and mourning for the martyred Hassan and Hussein.

monsoon: Seasonal wind prevailing in southern India; accompanied by heavy and continuous rainfall.

mosque: Muslim place of worship.

nautch: An East Indian exhibition of dancing, performed by professional dancing girls. It is clear from Aziz's references that they were also a higher class of prostitute.

nawab: (cf. nabob): A native governor or nobleman in India, or a wealthy, retired Anglo-Indian.

nullah: A river or stream; riverbed, ravine.

pargana (also **pergunnah**): A division of territory in India, comprising a number of villages, subdivision of a zillah.

peon: In India, a foot soldier, a native constable, an attendant or orderly; a footman or messenger.

pie: A small copper coin.

pujah (also **puja**): Ceremony of worship, an offering to the gods.

pukka: (from Hindi **pakka**) Cooked, ripe, mature; hence substantial, Permanent. Also: larger of two weights, hence of full weight, genuine, good, permanent, solid.

punkah: A portable fan generally made from the leaf of a palmyra palm; or a large swinging fan made of cloth stretched on a rectangular frame, suspended from the ceiling or rafters and worked by a cord.

punkah-wallah: Native Indian servant who works a punkah.

purdah: A curtain serving to screen women from the sight of men or strangers; the custom of secluding Indian women of rank.

raga: Musical composition, composed to be played at a certain hour and a certain season.

Raj: Sovereignty, rule, kingdom. Applied to British rule in India.

Rajah: Originally title given in India to kings or princes, later applied to petty chiefs.

rupee: The monetary unit of India.

saddhu: Indian holy man.

sahib: Originally: master, friend. Later, a respectful title used by natives of India in addressing an Englishman or other European.

sais (also **syce**): A servant who tends horses; a groom.

salaam: From the Muslim salutation "as-salaam alaikum"—Peace be upon you. Hence applied, in India, to a low bowing of head and body with the palm of the right hand placed on the forehead.

Sanskrit: Ancient and sacred language of India. Oldest known of the Indo-European languages.

sari: Long wrapping garment of cotton or silk, usually bright, worn by Hindu women.

shikars: Hunting, sport, shooting.

Shri: (usually **Sri**): Lord, a title given a deity

Sweepers: Harijan, or Untouchables, the lowest caste Hindus, often cleaners of latrines, hence the name.

tank: Artifical pond or lake.

tazia: Applied to a taboot; replica of Hussein and Hassan carried in the Mohurram procession, afterwards thrown into the water.

tiffin: A light midday meal, luncheon.

tonga: A light and small two-wheeled carriage or cart used in India.

topi: Stiff helmet-shaped hat to protect the head from the sun.

tum-tum: Anglo-Indian: a dog cart.

Urdu: Most common Hindustani dialect in India.

Viceroy: One who acts as governor of a country, in this case, India.

wallah: Hindu suffix indicating: pertaining or connected to. Rather like the suffix "-er" in English. Anglo-Indian: Man, fellow.

SECTION FIVE

Bibliography

Beer, J. B. *The Achievement of E. M. Forster.* London: Chatto & Windus, 1962.

Beer, J. B. and G. K. Das. *E. M. Forster: A Human Exploration.* London: The Macmillan Press, 1979.

Crews, F. C. *E. M. Forster: The Perils of Humanism.* Princeton: Princeton University Press, 1962.

Danièlou, Alain. *The Myths and Gods of India.* Rochester: Inner Traditions International, Ltd., 1985. (Originally published as *Hindu Polytheism.* New York: The Bollingen Foundation, 1964.)

Das, G. K. "A Passage to India: A Socio-Historical Study." In *A Passage to India: Essays in Interpretation.* ed. John Beer. London: The Macmillan Press, 1985.

Das, G. K. *E. M. Forster's India.* London: The Macmillan Press, Ltd., 1977.

Forster, E. M. *Aspects of the Novel.* New York: Harcourt Brace & Co., 1927.

——— *A Passage to India.* New York: Harcourt Brace Jovanovich, 1984.

Singer, Milton, ed. *Krishna: Myths, Rites, and Attitudes.* Honolulu: East-West Center Press, 1966. (Originally published by The University of Chicago Press.)

McDonell, Frederick P. W. *E. M. Forster.* Boston: Twayne Publishers, 1982. (Twayne's English Authors Series)

Schimmel, Annemarie. *Mystical Dimensions of Islam.* Chapel Hill: The University of North Carolina Press, 1975.

Stallybrass, Oliver, ed. Aspects of *E. M. Forster: Essays and Recollections for his Ninetieth Birthday.* New York: Harcourt, Brace & World, 1969.

Stone, Wilfred. *The Cave and the Mountain.* California: Stanford University Press, 1966.

Yeats-Brown, Francis. *The Lives of a Bengal Lancer.* New York: The Viking Press, 1930.

Yule, Col. Henry and A. C. Burrell. *Hobson-Jobson: A Glossary of Colloquial Anglo-Indian Words and Phrases, and of Kindred Terms, Etymological, Historical, Geographical and Discursive.* New Edition edited by William Crooke. Delhi: Munshiram Manoharial, 1968.

REA's **Test Preps**
The Best in Test Preparatio

- REA "Test Preps" are far **more** comprehensive than any other test preparation series
- Each book contains up to **eight** full-length practice exams based on the most recent exa
- **Every** type of question likely to be given on the exams is included
- Answers are accompanied by **full** and **detailed** explanations

REA has published over 60 Test Preparation volumes in several series. They include:

Advanced Placement Exams (APs)
Biology
Calculus AB & Calculus BC
Chemistry
Computer Science
English Language & Composition
English Literature & Composition
European History
Government & Politics
Physics
Psychology
Spanish Language
United States History

College Level Examination Program (CLEP)
American History I
Analysis & Interpretation of Literature
College Algebra
Freshman College Composition
General Examinations
Human Growth and Development
Introductory Sociology
Principles of Marketing

SAT II: Subject Tests
American History
Biology
Chemistry
French
German
Literature

SAT II: Subject Tests (continued)
Mathematics Level IC, IIC
Physics
Spanish
Writing

Graduate Record Exams (GREs)
Biology
Chemistry
Computer Science
Economics
Engineering
General
History
Literature in English
Mathematics
Physics
Political Science
Psychology
Sociology

ACT - American College Testing Assessment

ASVAB - Armed Service Vocational Aptitude Battery

CBEST - California Basic Educational Skills Test

CDL - Commercial Driver's License Exam

CLAST - College Level Academic Skills Test

ELM - Entry Level Mathematics

ExCET - Exam for Certification Educators in Texas

FE (EIT) - Fundamentals of Engineering Exam

FE Review - Fundamentals of Engineering Review

GED - High School Equivalency Diploma Exam (US & Canadi editions)

GMAT - Graduate Management Admission Test

LSAT - Law School Admission T

MAT - Miller Analogies Test

MCAT - Medical College Admiss Test

MSAT - Multiple Subjects Assessment for Teachers

NTE - National Teachers Exam

PPST - Pre-Professional Skills T

PSAT - Preliminary Scholastic Assessment Test

SAT I - Reasoning Test

SAT I - Quick Study & Review

TASP - Texas Academic Skills Program

TOEFL - Test of English as a Foreign Language

RESEARCH & EDUCATION ASSOCIATION
61 Ethel Road W. • Piscataway, New Jersey 08854
Phone: (908) 819-8880

Please send me more information about your Test Prep Books

Name _____

Address _____

City _____ State _____ Zip _____